Also by Ellen DeGeneres

My Point... And I Do Have One

The Funny Thing Is...

ELLEN DEGENERES

Seriously...I'm Kidding

GRAND CENTRAL
PUBLISHING

LARGE PRINT

Grand Central Publishing
Hachette Book Group
237 Park Avenue
New York, NY 10017

www.HachetteBookGroup.com

Book design by Fearn Cutler de Vicq

Printed in the United States of America

First Edition: October 2011

10   9   8   7   6   5   4   3   2   1

Grand Central Publishing is a division of Hachette Book Group, Inc.
The Grand Central Publishing name and logo is a trademark of
Hachette Book Group, Inc.

The publisher is not responsible for websites (or their content) that
are not owned by the publisher.

Library of Congress Cataloging-in-Publication Data

DeGeneres, Ellen.
    Seriously—I'm kidding / Ellen DeGeneres. — 1st ed.
        p. cm.
    ISBN 978-0-446-58502-6 (regular edition) — ISBN
978-1-4555-0415-2 (large print edition) 1. DeGeneres,
Ellen. 2. Comedians—United States—Biography. 3. Television
personalities—United States—Biography. I. Title.
    PN2287.D358A3 2011
    792.702'8092—dc23
    [B]
                                                    2011024930

To all my fans—

There's no joke here.

Thank you for your support.
Seriously . . . I'm not kidding.

Acknowledgments

I had a hard time deciding how to list and acknowledge all the important people in my life. I was going to list people in alphabetical order, but I didn't think that would be fair to Catherine Zeta-Jones. Then I thought maybe I should list everyone from shortest to tallest or thinnest to heaviest, but that didn't seem right either. So I decided to list everyone from smartest to dumbest. No, that's not true. This list is in no particular order. Just because someone is first doesn't mean they're the most important. It doesn't mean they're not the most important either. I am grateful for them all.

So in no particular order, 1'd like to thank:

Acknowledgments

My mother, my father, my brother, Craig Peralta, Eddy Yablans, Esther Newberg, Deb Futter, Eric Gold, Caryn Weingarten, Harley Neuman, Kevin Yorn, Hilary Estey McLoughlin, David McGuire, Ed Glavin, Mary Connelly, Andy Lassner, Lauren Pomerantz, Kevin Leman, Jason Gelles, and all my writers on my talk show.

Even though I did mention earlier that this list is in no particular order, there is one person who is the most important person in my life—my wife, Portia.

Thank you.

A Note from the Author

Dearest Reader,

Hello. How are you? That's great to hear. Listen, I want to thank you for buying this book. We're about to begin a beautiful journey together—one that is unique and special. I know a lot of you might watch my talk show, but communicating through a book is different than communicating through television. Like, on my talk show I tell you what's going on in my life and what I'm thinking about each day. But in this book, I'm going to tell you what's going on in my life and what I'm thinking about—you know what, I don't want to waste your time with silly comparisons.

But I bet a lot of you are probably thinking, Ellen (or "E" depending on how well we know one another), why are you writing another book after already proving yourself by penning two wildly, wildly successful tomes? Well the truth is, since I wrote my last book a lot has happened in my life. I got married. I got my own talk show. I started a record label. I became a CoverGirl. I was Dory. I won an Academy Award.[*] I won the Boston Marathon.[**] I started a compost heap.[***] And I was knighted by the Queen of England.[****]

[*] Unconfirmed at time of printing.

[**] Unable to pinpoint exact race placement and/or involvement in race at time of printing.

[***] In my neighbor's yard. Don't say anything.

[****] At time of printing, I was told this could never happen under any circumstances. But you know what I say, and this is an important life lesson, Readers—never say never.[†]

[†] I mentioned "never say never" to the British man I spoke with on the phone. He said in this case one could in fact say "never" because this can never happen, as I am not a "British" "citizen." So, unconfirmed at time of printing.

A Note from the Author

I've experienced a whole lot the last few years and I have a lot to share. So I hope that you'll take a moment to sit back, relax, and enjoy the words I've put together for you in this book. I think you'll find I've left no stone unturned, no door unopened, no window unbroken, no rug unvacuumed, no ivories untickled. What I'm saying is, let us begin, shall we?

Seriously...I'm Kidding

Writing This Book

Over the last year or so since I decided to write this book, people have been asking me how I have the time and why I chose to write it. The truth is, last June I was driving through a tunnel while I was on the phone with my agent and my cell service was spotty. I said, "I just got a great IKEA table for my breakfast nook." My agent thought I said, "I've got a great idea for my newest book."

By the time we figured out our hilarious misunderstanding I had signed a whole bunch of papers (who has time to read all those words?!) and I was under contract to write a book. Similarly, a few years ago, I told my agent, "I think

I got some fudge on my lapel," and he thought I said, "I want to be a judge on *American Idol.*" Since then I got a new phone. And I found out my agent's name is Marvin, not Blarvin.

But the real truth is, I'm glad I decided to write this book. I love writing and I do feel like I've learned a lot about life and love and other "L" words since I wrote my last book, and there are things I want to share with the world.

As it turns out, writing a book is hard. It's not as hard as mining coal or teaching teenagers to drive, I know that. But it is hard. I didn't think it would be so hard because I go on television every day and talk for an hour and I usually have plenty to say. Plus, I've already written other books—two as myself and dozens more under my pen name, Danielle Steel.

When I first sat down to write, I stared at the blank page and tried to think of some strategies for getting started. When I want a guest on my show to start talking and telling a good story, I ask them a question. So I asked myself a question that I would ask a guest: "When did you first fall in love with Tim McGraw?"

That didn't get me anywhere and I quickly realized I shouldn't ask myself questions that are so specific to Faith Hill.

So I asked myself a different question.

"What made you take on the role of *Precious*?"

That didn't work, either.

So then I began to think about you, the readers. Who are you? What are you doing? What are you wearing? (Not in a weird way.) I thought it would help to put myself in your shoes for a moment. It always helps to think about other people instead of just ourselves. Like, if you want to know what I'm doing right now, I'm driving to work with my top down. The roof of my convertible is up. I am wearing a beret—it helps me think and it makes me feel French. That is also why I'm pretending to smoke a straw, and that is probably why a bus full of tourists is staring at me.

So what would you like to hear about as my reader? I wondered. Perhaps you might like to hear about some of the highlights that have occurred throughout my life and career, but it's hard to know what highlights you would find exciting versus the highlights I think are exciting. For example, a few years ago I called my credit card company and got a late fee reversed that quite honestly I didn't think they'd reverse. That was a really big moment for me because you know how cranky some customer service representatives can be when they're having a bad day. But I don't know if that qualifies as the type of highlight you're looking to hear about.

I let my mind wander through some of the biggest moments in my life and then I realized what I needed to do. Since I don't know specific things about each and every one of you, except that a lot of you are probably brunettes, I decided to include a little something for everyone in this book. You're going to find some short stories for adults, coloring pages for kids, and many things for all ages in between. You'll also find self-help tips, some medical advice (from someone who has no medical background nor the authority to dole out medical advice), nutrition facts, and you might even learn how to be happier in your everyday lives. I hope you do.

ADDENDUM

There are a few things I wanted to include in this book but decided instead to save for my memoir. The following is a list of things you will not read about in this book:

- Details of my long-term relationship with Javier Bardem.
- My years spent in juvie.
- My early days as a pioneer of disco.
- My involvement with the Milli Vanilli lip-synching scandal of 1990.
- My recently discovered half-sister.
- The leaked sex tape.

CoverGirl

Beauty is in the eye of the beholder.
Beauty is only skin deep.
Beauty is not in the face; beauty is a
light in the heart.

Throughout my entire life, I have believed in these sentiments. I've believed that true beauty is not related to what color your hair is or what color your eyes are. True beauty is about who you are as a human being, your principles, your moral compass. And then in 2008 I was finally able to throw all that hogwash out the window because I was named the new face of CoverGirl cosmetics! Take a bite out of that, world! Check out these cheekbones! I'm a beauty queen! (This is where flashbulbs go off and I turn my head from side to side, posing like a supermodel. It was apparently "too expensive" and "not possible" to put mini lightbulbs in every book, so you're just gonna have to imagine it. I'm sorry.)

The truth is, I still believe that above all things physical, it is more important to be beautiful on the inside—to have a big heart and an open mind and a spectacular spleen. (Actually, most people's insides are disgusting. Even pretty people have very unattractive insides. Have you ever seen those surgery shows on Discovery? Not pretty.)

To me, beauty is about being comfortable in your own skin. It's about knowing and accepting who you are. I'm happy being who I am. I'm confident, I live honestly and truthfully, and I think that's why I was chosen as the first fifty-year-old, openly gay CoverGirl. It's just a bonus that I have devastatingly blue eyes.

But we really are a society that focuses so much on physical appearance. I realized this recently when I accidentally looked into one of those mirrors that magnify your face to five hundred times its actual size. They sell them at Bed Bath & Beyond in the "Things That Make You Feel Bad About Yourself" aisle. They're right next to the bathroom scales, usually on a shelf you're too short to reach. I'm sure you've all looked into one of them at some point. On one side, it's a totally normal mirror. And then if you turn it over to the other side, your face looks like the surface of the moon.

Portia and I have one in our shower. I never look in it because it's usually blocked by the person who washes me. But for some reason I looked in it one day and, oh Lordy, that is a horrible invention! Who invented that thing and why haven't they been jailed? Those things need to come with a warning. Car mirrors have warnings that say, "Objects are closer than they appear." Magnification mirrors should have warnings that say, "Objects are not as attractive as they appear."

They show you things you didn't know were there, that no one can possibly see. I looked at my hairline and I found a family of doves living in it. It was shocking. The only people who need to see things that close up are surgeons who are performing delicate operations and jewelers. That's it. No one is gonna see you the way you see yourself in those mirrors unless you're married to a surgeon or a jeweler and they come home from work still wearing that apparatus. "Honey, I'm home. Oh my goodness, your pores are huge!"

I don't know why we ever need to look into those. They're not accurate. They point out every single one of our flaws. We don't need that. That's why we have mothers. The fact of the matter is that everyone has flaws. No one is perfect, except for Penélope Cruz. Our flaws are what make us human. If we can accept them as part of who we are, they really don't even have to be an issue.

I feel the same way about age. I've never been someone to lie about my age. I don't understand it. Actually, I don't know how people can lie about their age anymore now that the Internet exists. Not only can people easily find out what year I was born, they can find out what time, what hospital, how long my mother was in labor. I wouldn't be surprised if there was footage on YouTube of the doctor spanking me. The only reason there isn't is because YouTube didn't exist when I was born.

Our age is something we have absolutely no control over; it's just a fact of who we are. I enjoy growing older and wiser and learning from my mistakes every single day. I'm happy, for example, that I no longer eat paste, like I did when I was twenty-four. And I'm happy that in a few years I'll be able to get half-price tickets to movies and museums. Considering how often I go to the movies and museums, I could save upward of thirty dollars a year.

When we were kids, all we wanted was to be older. When we were seven and a half and someone said we were only seven, we were furious. We probably even cried about it. Can you imagine doing that now as an adult? "This is Marsha. She's forty-two." "Forty-two and a half! You always forget the half! I'm practically forty-two and three-quarters!" I don't know at what age people stop wanting to be older. People seem to enjoy their twenties and thirties. It must be around forty, when you're "over the hill." I don't even know what that means and why it's a bad thing. When I go hiking and I get over the hill, that means I'm past the hard part and there's a snack in my future. That's a good thing as far as I'm concerned.

People seem to be shy about their age through their fifties and sixties, but then once they hit seventy or eighty, they start telling people again because it's such a huge victory to have made it that far. No one gets to one hundred and tells people they're only ninety-five. So I don't know why anyone has to lie about those middle years. We should celebrate every year that we made it through and every year that we're happier and healthier. Because honestly, that's the best-case scenario. And the bottom line is we are who we are—we look a certain way, we talk a certain way, we walk a certain way. I strut because I'm a supermodel, and sometimes I gallop for fun. When we learn to accept that, other people learn to accept us. So be who you really are. Embrace who you are. Literally. Hug yourself. Accept who you are. Unless you're a serial killer.

I know it seems easy and breezy for me to say, but trust me—it's okay to be you. If you had called me fifteen years ago and told me I was going to end up being a CoverGirl, I would have said, "No way" and "How'd you get this number?" But look at me now. I'm totally myself and I'm an internationally known, widely sought-after supermodel. I even went to Paris one time.

How to Be a Supermodel

Since I am a CoverGirl, I thought if any of you are interested in learning a little bit about modeling I could offer you some tips. I've sashayed down plenty of catwalks in my day—well, one. But I know what it takes to make an impression. So here are some suggestions, as long as you are willing to be fierce.

One: The Look
Always look like you're angry at the universe for making you too pretty.

Two: The Walk
Trot. Aggressively, like you're a horse that's trying to avoid puddles.

Three: The Squint

Squint like someone is bouncing sunlight off their watch and directly into your eyes.

Four: The Pout

Get those lips out there. Purse your lips like you're trying to sip out of a straw that someone keeps moving away from you.

Five: The Pose

Be mysterious. Always pose with one hand in your pocket as if to say, "I'm so mysterious, this hand in my pocket could be a hook hand. You don't know."

Six: The Breeze

Carry a giant oscillating fan with you at all times. No exceptions.

Now put it all together. Trot! Squint! Get the straw! Who's a pretty girl? You are. Keep trotting!

Stuff

I don't like clutter. I firmly believe that there is a place for everything and everything should be in its place. And I know there's a name for people like me: neat.

It is astounding to me how much stuff we all have. Our closets are full of stuff. Our drawers are full of stuff. Our stuff is piled on top of other stuff. And the older we get the more stuff we have because over the years we buy more and more stuff and we never want to let go of anything. Nowadays people are a little more aware of how much stuff they have because there's a bit of a social stigma if you have too much stuff. There's even a name for the people who have the most stuff. They're called hoarders. Back in the day they were just called grandmothers.

If you want to clean out your house and get rid of stuff, you can always do a good spring cleaning every year. Or you can do what I do. Move. I move a lot. I've moved about ten times over the past fifteen years. I don't move for the sole purpose of getting rid of stuff. I'm not crazy. I also move so that I never have to wash any windows. "Is that a smudge? Time to pack it up. Let's go."

When you're packing up a house, you're forced to decide what you really need versus what you can get rid of. You might have been holding on to cases and cases of empty glass jars, but once you have to pack them up and move them, you realize maybe you're not going to harvest your own honey.

My mama is similar to me in that she also likes to move a lot. Mama has moved thirty-two times since 1952. It's so funny because I remember sometimes I would come home from school and there would be a note on the door that said, "I moved. Try and find me!" And I would spend hours and hours trying to find the new house. Sometimes I would find it by nightfall but sometimes I wouldn't. Actually this is really funny—one time she accidentally forgot to leave a note and I had no idea she had even moved. I was living in the house with a beautiful Mexican family for about three months before I realized they weren't my cousins visiting from out of town. They were so nice. They called me "*Quien es, quien es,*" which I thought was a beautiful name.

Anyway, my mama might be similar to me as far as moving around goes, but as far as clutter is concerned she's a little different. When she moved into the house she lives in now (I think she's gonna stay there for a while—they say the thirty-second time is the charm), she made it a point to tell me how excited she was because she was going to downsize. She was getting rid of all the stuff she didn't need anymore and starting fresh in her new house. I was so proud of her. I went over to help her settle in and I assumed when I got there I wouldn't have to unpack much more than a pillow and a spoon. Not so.

Let me share with you all of the items Betty "I Am Downsizing" DeGeneres asked movers to wrap up, place in a box, seal up in the box, put in a van, and move into a whole new house so that I could cut open the box, take out the items, and unwrap them:

1. A three-hole punch.
2. A single-hole punch.
3. A VHS tape of *Abs of Steel*.
4. An unopened VHS tape of *Hip Hop Abs*.
5. A harmonica.
6. Another harmonica.
7. A third harmonica.
8. A rusty sifter.
9. A colander from 1953.
10. Biscuit cutters.

Many of those items have moved thirty-two times. And I should point a few things out. First of all, Mama moved into that house in 2010 not 1987, as the VHS tapes would have you believe.

Second of all, Mama is not in a blues band. She doesn't play the harmonica and even if she did, the ones I found in that box looked like they had been dug up next to some train tracks. If Mama put her mouth anywhere near them I would immediately take her for a tetanus shot. Thirdly, Mama does not cook or bake or prepare food in any way. I don't know what sort of imaginary biscuits she thinks she's going to cut.

I could not believe how much stuff my mama still had, but it's because we all justify holding on to things. We do this especially with clothing. We all have so many things in our closets that we never wear but we convince ourselves to keep just in case we ever need to paint. We don't paint, we won't paint, but we have dozens of old Wham! T-shirts just in case.

A lot of people hold on to clothing just for the sentimental value. They say, "I can't get rid of this jacket. I love it. I wore it on my first cruise." Of course you love it. You bought it. But it doesn't fit you anymore and the shoulder pads make you look like a 1980s football player who loved the color salmon.

I'm guilty of it, too. I still have the shirt I wore my first time on Johnny Carson. Only now I use it as a tablecloth at dinner parties. It was very blousy.

We're always worried that we're going to get rid of something and then it's going to come back in fashion. But even if it does—and I assure you that paisley jumpsuit you've been holding on to won't—they always make a tiny tweak so that it's a little bit different so we have to buy the updated version.

One year, big collars are in and the next year they make collars an eighth of an inch shorter. So we go out and buy the collar that's an eighth of an inch shorter because heaven forbid someone sees us walking around town with last year's collar. As if strangers on the street are going to come up to us and measure our collars. "Oh no. She's wearing last year's collar, everyone! She's wearing last year's collar!"

It's not just clothing we hold on to. It's old electronics and old furniture and I'll tell you one thing I recently discovered in my own home—lotion. Portia hoards lotion. I don't know how it took me so long to notice but she has bottles and bottles of lotion. There are some lined up on the counter, some in baskets under the sink. She has cheap ones from drugstores and real fancy ones from the Sheraton and the Holiday Inn.

She has every kind of lotion there is—and there's a lot. There's lotion for your face, lotion for your hands, lotion for your feet, lotion for your body. Why? What would happen if you put hand lotion on your feet? Would your feet get confused and start clapping?

Each kind says it has something special in it for your skin—aloe, shea butter, coconut, cocoa butter, vanilla, lemon extract. That's not lotion. That's one ingredient short of a Bundt cake.

Don't get me wrong. I like lotion. I use a moisturizer on my face. I have to—it's my moneymaker. And I like to use hand lotion. I shake a lot of hands and I want people to experience my suppleness. But hand lotion is tricky. You have to know exactly how much to put on. You don't want to overdo it. Portia once put too much on and got stuck in the bathroom for an hour trying to turn the doorknob. Then I had to remind her we have a door that slides.

My point is everyone who has buckets and buckets of lotion should get rid of all the lotion they don't use anymore. And by everyone I do mean Portia. Or at least she should think about combining all the half bottles into one giant bottle so we can get rid of some stuff and she can smell like a baby eating a cucumber in an orange grove. I hope she reads this.

I really do think it's important to let go of things and give things away, to declutter and get out from under that pile of papers and old cereal boxes and harmonicas. It's cathartic. It's freeing. Plus you can get good money for some stuff on eBay. A "vintage" colander goes for just under $3.50. Mama's gonna be rich!

Personally Speaking

I spend a lot of time exploring my body. Hang on, that doesn't sound quite right. What I mean to say is, I like to constantly be in touch with my own body. Okay, that's not right, either. My body is a wonderland. I don't even know why I just said that.

What I'm trying to say is that as I've gotten older I've started to pay closer attention to my body and to my physical well-being. I think we all have to do that as we get older. We have to check ourselves out, literally, to make sure nothing has appeared or disappeared or grown or shrunk or tightened or loosened or sagged or ulcered or bulged or inflamed. I really hope you're not eating.

Once we hit forty and fifty years old, our bodies go through a lot of changes. Even if we're in really good shape (read: I have buns of steel) things start to slow down. Our metabolism slows down, our reflexes slow down, sometimes we become slightly more forgetful. I don't want to alarm anyone who isn't there yet, but you should know that a day will come when you leave your keys in the freezer and try to start your car with a bagel. You should also know that studies have shown that after age fifty there is a 97 percent chance you will pull your groin while putting on a bathing suit. It's a proven fact. You can do the research on your own time.

I actually pulled my groin once a few years ago. I don't even know how I did it. All I know is when it happened I was right in the middle of auditioning for the Rockettes and it ruined everything. The problem with pulling your groin, besides pulling your groin, is that there isn't a delicate way to treat it. Whenever I pull a muscle in my back, I get a massage to make it feel better. When you pull a muscle in your groinal region, it's much trickier. You can't ask a stranger to massage it. That's why I had to ask my gardener to do it. And I'll be honest—at first it was awkward. But then it was beautiful.

We have to take care of ourselves as we age and that includes getting procedures done that are invasive, uncomfortable, and at times what many would refer to as "third date territory." One of those procedures is a colonoscopy. I had my first routine colonoscopy after I turned fifty. I'm sure you all know what it entails, but if you don't I'll explain it as best I can. Basically, a colonoscopy is a procedure where a camera starts downtown and travels uptown on the C train. In Los Angeles, they do it a little bit differently. They attach cameras to teeny, tiny paparazzi who head up there and take thousands of pictures of your colon that later end up on TMZ.

I didn't know exactly what to expect when I went in for my colonoscopy. First of all, because of my work schedule, I had to get mine done on a Saturday. Luckily, there's a little kiosk in the mall that does colonoscopies and ear piercing on the weekends.

The first thing I had to do when I got there was put on a gown. I think it was a Zac Posen. I don't normally wear gowns, but this was a beautiful one—open in the back and slightly off the shoulder. They made me take everything off except my socks. I guess they let you keep those on so that you don't feel totally naked. As it turns out, even with socks on you still feel totally and completely naked. I don't know what they're thinking. Socks or no socks, all the important parts are still out and about.

After I was in my gown and socks, the doctor came in and greeted me. She was also wearing a gown so I tried to make a joke like, "Hey, isn't it embarrassing that we're wearing the same gown?" She laughed but she was holding a needle at the time, so it suddenly felt like a scene from *Misery*. Right away she started to give me sleepy-time drugs. That's the medical term. And all I remember after the sleepy-time drugs is saying, "I gotta get—" and that's it. I was out for the rest of the procedure. When you wake up, it's a little disorienting. You're not sure where you are. Katie Couric is there with a film crew. It's jarring. But it's necessary and I'm glad I did it.

Another routine procedure that every woman needs to get is a mammogram. Now, the word "mammogram" makes it sound like it's going to be a fun experience. You think a cute little grandma is going to show up at your door to sing you a happy birthday song or something. Unfortunately, that is not the case. A mammogram is less like a fun song and more like an industrial-strength panini press.

The difference between a colonoscopy and a mammogram—well, there are a few differences obviously. One takes place above the equator and one takes place below it. But the other difference is that with a mammogram you are fully aware of what is going on. You don't need any drugs to knock you out because it's not a painful procedure. It's just uncomfortable and awkward, especially given the fact that you are standing face to face with the technician working the machine. At least, it's awkward for me anyway because inevitably I have to make small talk. "Yep, I do dance a lot... No, not all the time... Well, I'm a big fan of your mom, so thank you, that's nice to hear."

I cannot believe they haven't yet come up with a better screening process than the mammogram. If a man had to put his special parts inside a clamp to test him for anything, I think they would come up with a new plan before the doctor finished saying, "Put that thing there so I can crush it."

I'm getting away from my point. My point is, these tests are very important. And I don't mind telling you all about my groin, my colon, and my breasts if it means helping you take care of yourself. I just thought of something else I could share with you. Would you like to hear about one of my moles? No. Okay. Moving on.

The Secret of Life

K ale.

The Secret of Life—Part Two

Okay, there might be more to the secret of life than kale. (Although it really is an incredible leaf. One serving of kale has 88 percent of your daily value of vitamin C. That's the nutritional element of the book I was referring to earlier.)

People are constantly searching for the secret of life. In terms of what people spend their time searching for, it goes sunglasses, the secret of life, the fountain of youth, car in the mall parking lot, cell phone, keys, contact lenses, love. We all spend time searching for the secret of life because we think it will bring us closer to the one thing we all want—the one thing that, no matter what we do in our lives or where we go or who we marry, we all aspire to have. It's the most important thing in the world: money. No, I'm sorry, not money. Happiness. That's what I meant—happiness. And once you find happiness, you've pretty much uncovered the secret.

Some people believe that to find happiness, you should live each day of your life as if it's your last because that way you will appreciate every single moment you have. Other people believe that you should live each day as if it's your first because then every day can be the beginning of a new journey. Those are conflicting ideas, and I know it can be confusing. Do you live each day as if it's your first or your last? Either way you should probably have a diaper on.

If you lived each day like it's your first, you would constantly be discovering the world like babies do. Babies have an incredible sense of wonder. They are in awe of everything around them, from mirrors to squeaky toys to their own hands. The simplest things are mesmerizing to them. Adults are sometimes mesmerized by their own hands but it's usually under very different circumstances, when they're attending music festivals in the desert.

That's why it's so refreshing for me to be around my two-year-old niece. Everything excites her right now because she's experiencing so many things for the very first time. She's learning how to walk and talk. Recently we let her drive on the freeway for the first time. She went wild for it.

For some reason as we get older, we lose that sense of wonder. We get jaded. I don't know when it happens exactly, but I think it's sometime between finding out the tooth fairy doesn't exist and realizing the *Real Housewives* are neither real nor housewives.

It could also be that we're desensitized. Between YouTube and reality television and Cinemax After Dark, we've pretty much seen it all. There are very few things that wow us anymore. A child will see something as simple as a garage door opening and it's literally all they will talk about for weeks. As an adult, we will see a human person ride a bike, catapult over eighteen cars that are on fire, land on a skateboard, slide down a ramp, and end up in the backseat of a taxi, and be like, "Yeah, that was all right. But did you see the guy who pogo sticked over thirty-eight grandmothers?"

I'm not saying we need to live like babies in every way. I mean, sure, it would be great to get carried around in a papoose. Who wouldn't want that? But I am glad I'm potty trained and not always trying to eat my feet like babies do.

I just wish we could hold on to that sense of wonder because sometimes we don't notice some of the most incredible things in the world. We walk by beautiful flowers and trees every day without looking at them. We rush through our day without even saying hi to most of the people we see. We take a lot for granted, and I think that's why some people say it's better to live each day as our last. That way we might start appreciating more things around us. Either that or we would immediately quit our jobs to go live in a yurt.

If we lived each day as our last, I bet we'd all be a lot more honest with people, because we wouldn't have to care what people think anymore. We would meet a friend for lunch and blurt out, "Hey, that's an ugly hat!" Or tell a police officer, "If you thought that was speeding, sir, you should've seen what I was doing earlier! I think it was the fastest I've ever driven." Or if you break up with someone you would finally tell them, "I just want you to know, it's not me. It's you."

There would be nothing to lose, and because of that you would probably take a lot more chances in life. I think it's important to take risks. That doesn't mean you have to do something crazy like jump out of a plane or scale an ice-covered mountain using only your fingers, a short piece of rope, and a nail file. I don't know what makes people see sharp cliffs and say, "I'd like to dangle from that." Obviously, if you're into that sort of thing go for it, but if you're not, you can start small. Eat an apple without washing it first. Answer your phone even though the number calling is "unknown."

Wait only twenty-seven minutes to swim after you eat. Do whatever you think is risky.

When you take risks you learn that there will be times when you succeed and there will be times when you fail, and both are equally important. It's hard to understand failure when you're going through it, but in the grand scheme of things it's good to fall down—not because you're drunk and not near stairs.

But it's failure that gives you the proper perspective on success. When I came out of the closet on my sitcom I knew it was a risk, but I took the risk and look what happened. It got canceled. Not the point. The point is, I got back on my horse—when I found out my sitcom got canceled, I happened to be riding one of those toy horses outside the supermarket—and I pushed forward. I said, "You'll show them, Ellen!" And I did another sitcom. Guess what happened? That got canceled, too. Not the point, either. The real point is that I kept going and now I appreciate my success more than I could have ever imagined. I look back on the days of doing stand-up in a basement for three friends—well, one friend and two mice. Okay, three mice. And I am so proud of where I am today. So let that be a lesson, kids who get an F in math. Ellen says you're doing the right thing. You're welcome, parents.

When you really think about it, it doesn't matter if you choose to live each day as your first or your last. You could live each day as your second or third so all the gunk you're born with is out of your eyes. Or you could live each day as your 912th or 15,337th. I actually remember that day in my life so clearly. I was in my forties and I needed a break from everything in my life, so I decided to get away. I went to Jamaica and I spent some time thinking about my life and what I wanted and I ended up learning how to get my groove back. You know what? I'm sorry. I'm thinking of *How Stella Got Her Groove Back*.

But what's important is that you enjoy and appreciate every day, and that's something you can accomplish by just living in the moment. Don't look behind you. Unless someone yells, "Look out behind you!" Then you should definitely look behind you because there's a good chance a Frisbee is being thrown at your head or, if you're in a movie, an attractive teenage vampire is about to attack you.

Otherwise, don't look back and don't spend too much time worrying about the future. Stay in the present. There are a few ways to do that. Stop and smell the roses. Wake up and smell the coffee. Enjoy the sweet smell of success. I guess just keep taking big whiffs of stuff because it seems like the more we smell, the happier we are going to be. You know what I mean.

Thunderclap: A Short Short Story

It was a dark and stormy night. The streets were empty. They seemed sad almost and hollow. The wind was howling and the rain was pouring down upon the rooftop so loud that Papa could barely hear the sound of his teakettle. Eventually, the storm passed and normal activity resumed.

Journal Entries

I usually like to keep my private matters private, but I thought I could make an exception this one time to share some of the journal entries I've written since 2003, right around the time my last book came out. Please enjoy a little insight into my personal musings over the last several years.

May 30, 2003

Dear Journal,

Remember that movie called *Finding Nemo* that I told you I worked on years and years ago? Well it came out today and guess what—it set the record for best opening day ever of an animated movie! I'm so proud to have been a part of it. I wouldn't be surprised if Pixar called me today to say they want to make a sequel. This is great. This is really, really great. What a wonderful, wonderful, perfect situation this is, Journal.

August 1, 2003

Journal,

Finding Nemo is now the highest-grossing animated movie of all time! Can you believe it?! Hang on, my phone's ringing. It's probably Pixar telling me they want to make a sequel! Bye, Journal! Talk to you again when I'm rich!

August 2, 2003

Journal,

That phone call wasn't about *Finding Nemo* 2, but I'm sure they'll call any minute. The call was about my new talk show! That's another thing I'm so excited about. It starts in about a month. I have to start thinking about what I want to wear on my first show and how I'm gonna get my hair did. Just thinking about it makes me want to dance up and down aisles for some reason! Anyway, I'll let you know when Pixar comes a-knockin'! Should be any second now.

September 8, 2003

Dear Journal,

Big day today. My talk show premiered on TV! Wow. I think this is gonna be really fun. People seemed to like it and I'm really proud of it. I don't know what my schedule is going to be like over the next few months and years, but don't worry, I'm still gonna try and write in here every single day.

February 25, 2007

Journal,

I just finished hosting the Oscars. I am currently experiencing an indescribable feeling. It's joy mixed with relief mixed with the smell of Clint Eastwood's after-shave. I can't believe I just hosted the

Academy Awards! I'm headed to the after party now. I'm sure it'll be a quiet, tame night. Just kidding. It's about to get crazy up in here. I have a feeling my three-piece suit will be down to one piece in about an hour, Journal, if you understand what I'm saying.

August 16, 2008

Dear Journal,

Today was the happiest day of my life. I got married. I am soooooooooooooooooooooooo happy. You can tell how happy I am based on how many "O"s I used. I've never used that many "O"s. Portia and I got married and exchanged vows in front of a small group of our friends and family. It was a perfect day.

May 16, 2009

Journal,

Today I gave the commencement speech at Tulane University in my hometown of New Orleans. I had a great time and I think I gave those kids a lot of great advice. I can't believe they let me do that even though I didn't go to no college. I meant to, but I totally forgot. I think I made my mama very proud today by making one of her dreams for me come true. I finally wore a gown.

January 26, 2010

Dear Journal,

Today is my birthday. I had a great day today and I'm so excited for this year. I have so much to look forward to. *American Idol* is starting up soon. I can't wait. I think I'm gonna want to do it forever.

March 15, 2010

Journal,

I'm on a sugar cleanse. I haven't had any sugar in over three weeks. I think I'm experiencing withdrawal. Today I screamed at a plant. I don't know why I decided to do this. It's crazy. There's sugar in everything. Did you know that? Every-thing. Even cupcakes. All right, I have to go, Journal. You're being a jerk.

May 26, 2010

J,

Big news. I'm starting a record label. I love music and I love discovering new artists. I won't be any different though now that I'm going to be a mogul. I'll still be the same old Ellen. Oh, I gotta bounce. My pimpmo-bile is outside. Look at those rims! Holla!

July 27, 2010

Journal,

What an exciting day. Remember I told you about all that gold I mailed in for cash? Guess what! The money arrived today. I got $1.24!

August 16, 2010

Dear Journal,

Today Portia and I celebrated our two-year wedding anniversary. When I got home from work Portia [OMITTED].

September 8, 2010

Journal,

I made my Broadway debut tonight in the Big Apple! I starred in a show called *Promises, Promises* alongside my supporting cast, Kristin Chenoweth and Sean Hayes. It was so much fun, but guess what, Journal? I think I caught the theater bug. Literally. There was a roach in my dressing room the size of my fist. New York City is filthy.

January 1, 2011

Happy 2011, Journal! Had a great New Year's Eve. Set a new record and managed to stay up until 9:30. It was craaaaazy, Journal.

January 18, 2011

Hey Journal,

I watched *The Biggest Loser* tonight. That show is so good. I can't stop crying. I don't know how they do it. I'm crying so much I have mascara running down my face. And I'm not even wearing mascara. This show is powerful.

May 25, 2011

Dear Journal,

Today was the very last episode ever of *The Oprah Winfrey Show*. Wow. I can't believe it. I don't know how her show got canceled. So many people loved it. But you know what this means? Now that Larry King retired, Oprah's moving on, and Regis quit, all of television will be mine! Hahahahaha!

June 24, 2011

Journal,

I'm about to turn my new book in to the publisher. Writing a book is hard. I thought it was mostly going to be journal entries like this, but it turns out they need more to fill a book. I wish it could be all journal entries. Anyway, I'm gonna send the book in and then probably head to the movies. You know what comes out today, Journal? *Cars* 2. Isn't that great? A sequel to a hit animated movie. I'm so, so, so happy for them.

Important Words

Now this is a very difficult chapter for me to write. This chapter, chapter ten, is my favorite chapter in one of my favorite books so I feel an enormous amount of pressure to make it spectacular. There are other books I've read where chapter ten was not that great at all. But I prefer not to tell you to which book I'm referring. Maybe the author of that book failed to read the chapter in the book I aforementioned.

I don't know if "aforementioned" is a word or if it's correctly used here. But whenever I feel stress or pressure of any kind I try to use big, important words. It makes me feel better and more powerful. Like, if I get pulled over for speeding I usually say something like, "Mr. (or Mrs. or Ms. depending on the situation, of course) Gentleman Enforcer of the Legal Government Principles, I am en route to my appendectomy." And then they usually say something like, "License and registration." And then I say, "Cacophony!" And then they usually write me a ticket.

I don't know why bigger words seem like they're more important. Really all words are important, even small words like "the" or "it" or "a" or "or," for that matter. You can't form a sentence without those words. Let me try to make a sentence without using any of those words just to make a point.

See? I can't.

Well, I guess technically "I can't" is a sentence that doesn't use "the" or "it" or "a" or "or" but you understand what I'm trying to say. All those small words are just as important as big words. I say it all the time about words and only words—it's not the size that counts. It's the way you use them in sentences, paragraphs, and slam poetry.

Some authors try to be all show-offy with fancy sentences. And I could do that if I really wanted to. It's not like I don't know all those rarely used big, fancy, ostentaneous words, too. Of course I do. And if that's what it takes for a book to win a Pulitzer or some grand literary prize I guess I could throw a sentence or two in. Why not? I'll do it right now.

One day my domesticated feline Charlie was unequivocally euphoric. I deducted this based on my astute observation of her level of loquaciousness while she hurriedly pursued her high-pitched squeakable toy rodent of the species *Mouseous*.

See? Easy. Here is another example:

Women are supposed to be very calm generally, but women feel just as men feel. They need exercise for their faculties, and a field for their efforts, as much as their brothers do; they suffer from too rigid a restraint, too absolute a stagnation, precisely as men would suffer; and it is narrow-minded in their more privileged fellow-creatures to say that they ought to confine themselves to making pudding and knitting stockings, to playing on the piano and embroidering bags. It is thoughtless to condemn them, or laugh at them, if they seek to do more or learn more than custom has pronounced necessary for their sex.

Okay, that was from *Jane Eyre*. I can't keep this charade up for a whole chapter. That *Jane Eyre* is really good, though, isn't it?

Family

We are family. I got all my sisters with me.
We are family. Get up everybody and sing.
—Sister Sledge

A few years ago I received a letter from a genealogist at the New England Historic Genealogical Society. At first I thought it was a letter from my lady doctor, but then someone told me "genealogy" means "family."

They wanted to know if I was interested in learning about my lineage. Up until that point in my life, I hadn't thought much about my family history. All I knew for sure was that I was born in Metairie, Louisiana, and I came out of my mama's belly button.

But as soon as I received the letter I started thinking about my past and my ancestors. Who am I? Where am I from? Why do I love hummus so much? So I asked the genealogists to do some research for me and they found out some very interesting facts.

They told me I am related to a whole bunch of celebrities, and not just in a Kevin Bacon sort of way. I mean actually related to. First of all, I found out I'm married to Portia de Rossi, which is amazing. She is beautiful and one of the nicest people I've ever met.

I also found out that I am tenth cousins once removed from Academy Award–winning actress Halle Berry. That's a pretty obvious one. Look at us. We're like twins. People are probably always passing her on the street, yelling, "Ellen, dance!"

I am also a distant cousin of Richard Gere, so now there are two reasons we can't date. I am eighth cousins nine times removed from

George Washington, which explains why I cannot tell a lie and I love to wear powdered wigs. And, most important of all, I'm royalty. I am fifteenth cousins with the future queen of England, Kate Middleton, which makes it a lot less weird that I have everyone who works for me call me Your Royal Highness.

Actually, I found out that my ancestors date all the way back to fifteenth-century England. That's like when Big Ben was just a tiny little baby Ben. I have relatives with names like Jean Laurent de Generes and Jean Baptiste de Generes, which are really fun to say. And I'm a descendant of William Brewster, who came over on the *Mayflower*. I assume that's why I'm so attracted to a shoe with a buckle.

It's exciting to find out what our roots are. Knowing where we come from explains so much about who we are. Plus, it gives us so many more people to borrow money from.

What's interesting when you really think about where we all come from and how different our pasts might be is that if you were to peer into the window of any house on any street during a big family holiday celebration, you would most likely see many of the same scenes. You would also risk getting arrested for trespassing, but still you would see that all of our families are very much the same. No matter where we're from or to whom we're related or how our pasts have impacted our current lives, every family gathering tends to go the same way.

First, you hope that your favorite aunt invites you to her house for the holidays because she has the finished basement with the nice pool table. She's not going to. Instead, everyone is going to your uncle's who has four pit bulls and an indoor skate ramp made out of recycled beer bottles.

As soon as you get there you get stuck talking to your brother-in-law's brother. You have nothing to talk about so you start with "Wow, I haven't seen you since you were on *Cops*." Immediately your mom grabs you and says, "You weren't supposed to mention *Cops*! Why did you mention *Cops*?!"

Then you apologize for mentioning *Cops*. Somehow in the apology, you make a joke like, "Well at least you weren't on *To Catch a Predator*, right?" Another apology is made.

Then cousin Pam shows up with her famous corn casserole that is famous for all the wrong reasons. You know the first thing she's going to want to do is play the guitar and sing about peace, so you decide to go outside for some fresh air even though it's four degrees and snowing and you forgot to pack a coat. Two seconds later, nine kids follow you outside to pelt you with snowballs and when you don't throw any back at them they start to call you names and make you feel bad that your skin turns so red in the cold. It's not your fault, you've always had sensitive skin and there's nothing wrong with being sensitive.

You tell the kids that but it doesn't go well at all so you head back inside and ask if you can do anything to help because you're polite, and also because your mom is giving you the "You better ask if you can help, I didn't raise you to just stand there and do nothing" look. You hope the answer will be no, but your aunt says, "Sure! I haven't made the sweet potato pie yet. You can do that!"

Then you panic because you've never known the difference between a sweet potato and a yam and both are on the counter, and if you start making a yam pie you'll never hear the end of it.

So you start making a yam pie. Luckily, people are distracted by a dozen grown men screaming in the living room because little Timmy unplugged the TV just as a football team was scoring a touchdown.

Timmy starts to cry. The dogs start to bark. Everyone finally sits down to eat. The wine will start flowing and so will the secrets. Guess what? Mom's pregnant. Guess what else? So is Dad. He can do that now.

You scarf down your meal and head home wondering if everyone's family is that crazy. The answer is a resounding yes.

But we should be grateful for them because without our family—the ancestors we descend from, the cousins we see once a year, the loves of our lives we see every day—life is pretty boring. You don't have to believe me, but you should. I'm royalty.

What Would Jesus Do?

I don't know if you've read a magazine lately or gone online or watched TV or visited a mall—I don't know what you do in your spare time and frankly it isn't any of my business. But if you have done any of those things, you've probably been asked to participate in an opinion poll. Opinion polls have become incredibly popular. People love them. I know because I read that in an opinion poll.

Lately it seems that every magazine has a poll, every tabloid has a poll, every Internet site, every bedroom in my house. That's a different kind of pole, but I'm just sharing with you. And I have to say—I'm not sure that all these polls are totally necessary. A lot of them ask the same questions. Which couple is cuter? Do you like her dress? Do you like his shirt? Who wore it better? Are they too skinny, too fat, too pretty, too ugly, too tall, too short, too hairy, not hairy enough?

Many of them ask questions that not only seem unnecessary but, to use a technical term, are also bonkers. I won't say the name of the magazine (it sounds like "Pin Style") I stole from my dentist's office but there was a poll in it that asked readers, "How far will you take the season's hot shade of green?" Thirty-nine percent of people said "All the way," 37 percent said "Halfway," and 24 percent said "Just a hint."

Now, here's my first question: What?! How far will you take the season's hot shade of green? What does that mean? What does it mean to take green "all the way"? Like, to the prom? Are you going to settle down and have children with the color green? And look how close it is between "All the way" and "Halfway." There's only a 2 percent difference. I'm surprised we didn't hear about that on the evening news.

I read another poll in a different magazine that I cannot and will not name even if you beg me to. (It sounds a lot like "Clamor.") It asked readers, "Hot pink dress—is it a do or a don't?" Now here's my question about this poll: Who cares? If you want to wear a pink dress, wear a pink dress. It doesn't matter what other people think. One hundred percent of the people polled could say a pink dress is a "do" and guess what? I still ain't wearing one.

I've been in these magazines and it's always an awkward thing to open one up and see yourself compared to a bunch of random people. It's like, "Who wore it better? Ellen or Heidi Klum?" And obviously when you put the two of us side by side, it's just not fair to Heidi.

They go after everyone in those polls. I actually think if Jesus were alive today, there would be polls about him in *Us Weekly*. "Who wore this flowy gown better? Jesus or J. Lo?" "Jesus's sandals—hot to trot or heavens no?" "Do you think Jesus should cut his hair?" Fifty-four percent of readers say yes, Jesus should cut his hair. And of course that would be followed by

"Should Jesus cut his hair into a mullet or buzz cut?"

All these polls do is make everyone so judgmental. And I don't believe in judgment. Unless it's judgment of judgment. I don't think someone has to "wear something better" or have a better hairstyle. That's why the word "different" exists in our language. (I don't know why the word "mustache" exists, though. Can't we just call it lip hair?)

We all spend so much time comparing ourselves to each other. Everyone is running around trying to keep up with the Joneses. Who are the Joneses anyway? Why are we trying to keep up with them? I'm sure they're not perfect. We don't need to keep up with them. It's hard enough to keep up with the Kardashians.

And people compare everything. It's not just clothing. It's who has a bigger house, who drives a faster car, who has a better job. People compare their bodies to other people, and not only that, they compare what's on their bodies. Have you ever gotten a bruise or a scratch or a paper cut and shown someone else what happened? People immediately start stripping off their clothing to compare injuries.

I once went into work and showed some producers a little bruise I got. The next thing I knew it was like *Girls Gone Wild* in my office. People were lifting up their shirts, rolling up their pants. Socks were coming off. "You think that's bad—I walked into a tree yesterday!" "I banged my hip on a car door!" "I sat on a fork!" Don't need to see it.

People were showing me scars and beauty marks that were not at all beautiful. I'm gonna tell you all right now—even if your beauty mark is in the shape of a prize ribbon, I don't need to see it. (Same goes for stretch marks, ladies. When you say "Look what my kids did to me," I expect to see gum in your hair, not your whole midsection. And no, I will not rub cocoa butter on it.)

Anyway, all I'm saying is I don't see the sense in comparing ourselves to other people all the time. It's not about being better than anyone else or having nicer things or bigger fork marks on your behind.

I personally like being unique. I like being my own person with my own style and my own opinions and my own toothbrush. I think it's so much better to stand out in some way and to set yourself apart from the masses. It would be so boring to look out into the world and see hundreds of people who look and think exactly like me. If I wanted that, I could just sit in front of a mirror and admire my own reflection all day. That's already how I spend my mornings. I don't need to spend all of my time doing that.

And who's to say what's better or worse anyway? Who's to even say what's normal or average? We're all different people and we're allowed to be different from one another. If someone ever says you're weird, say thank you. And then curtsy. No, don't curtsy. That might be too weird. Bow. And tip your imaginary hat. That'll show them.

Haiku

Haiku sounds like I'm
Saying hi to someone named
Ku. Hi, Ku. Hello.

Stretching

There's one thing that should be essential to everyone's daily routine. I'm sorry, two things: watching my talk show and stretching. Feel free to stretch while you watch my talk show, if you think it's possible to take your eyes off me for even a second.

Stretching can apply to so many different areas of our lives. Not only should we literally stretch our bodies so that things are less likely to snap off, we should also stretch our minds. I think it's so important to keep our minds active and to constantly be learning new things. We shouldn't just stop at high school. I mean, technically I did. But you understand what I'm saying.

There are a lot of different ways to keep our minds active. A lot of people do crossword puzzles. Those are great for stimulating your brain. And other people love doing those really complicated and confusing puzzles where you have to place all the numbers and they have to add up. What's that called? Oh yeah, math.

I like to stretch my mind by reading and writing and watching educational TV shows like *The Bachelor* to learn the complex mating rituals of heterosexuals.

Portia recently decided to learn something new. She taught herself how to cook. She didn't take any lessons or classes or anything. She just figured it out on her own. And I know what you're thinking—uh-oh. But she's really good at it. Cooking isn't an easy skill to learn. It can be very dangerous. There's fire, there's steam, there are sharp, sharp knives. Portia is down to three fingers but she never gave up and that's why I love her.

I think it's great that she started to cook. Mostly because I can't. And it's nice to have one person in the relationship who cooks because that way we can share responsibilities in the kitchen, like a lot of couples do. Portia cooks and I clean. Just kidding. I don't clean. That's gross.

But I do think it's great that she was so excited to learn something new. I recommend it to everybody. Learn a new instrument. Learn to paint. Learn puppetry. Or you can just learn new facts. I can teach you a few things right now that you might not know. First of all, did you know that a snail can sleep for three years? That's why they move so slowly when they're awake. They're groggy. Did you know that raccoons have such nimble fingers they can not only open garbage can lids and turn doorknobs, they can untie shoelaces? Now you know why they're so good at putting on eyeliner.

Doesn't it feel nice to stretch your mind a little bit? Now that you've done that, it's time to move on to your body. Yoga is a great way to stretch your body. I try to do it every morning because it's a great way to start the day. It gives me a lot of energy and now that I've been doing it for a while I'm pretty good at it. My downward dog is so excellent, I can't show it on daytime television.

There are all different kinds of yoga. There's power yoga. There's Bikram yoga, which makes you sweat a lot because it's done in very hot rooms. You can always tell who does Bikram yoga because they're stinky. But all yoga is based on Hatha yoga, which is what I do, and Hatha yoga is based on watching animals stretch in nature. I know what you're thinking. "Ellen, I've seen my dog stretch out in certain ways to clean himself and I don't want to do that." That's not the part yoga focuses on.

The word "yoga" literally means "uniting," because when you're doing it you're uniting your mind and your body. You can tell this almost immediately because your mind will be thinking, "Ouch, that hurts," and your body will say, "I know." And your mind will think, "You have to get out of this position." And your body will say, "I agree with you, but I can't right now. I think I'm stuck."

Another thing that is great for stretching out your mind and body is meditation. It helps improve your memory and it increases blood flow. It forces you to calm down and relax. There are a lot of different ways to meditate. You can do it by yourself, or you can do it with other people. I'm still talking about meditation. You can do it anywhere. All you have to do is close your eyes. So you probably shouldn't do it while you're driving or operating heavy machinery, but otherwise you're good to go.

Meditation requires a lot of focus and sometimes it is easy to get distracted. I've tried taking classes because I think it's easier to meditate with other people. Being surrounded by good energy helps me focus and find positivity and happiness. But even then, I always want to open my eyes. Especially because there's incense burning and I always think the room is on fire. So instead of focusing on my inner joy, I focus on trying to remember where the closest exits are. At some point, I do tend to open my eyes for a second just to see if the room's on fire. Of course it isn't but when my eyes are open I see two other people with their eyes open and I wonder how long they've had them open. Then

I notice the giant gong and I think, "I wonder what happened to *The Gong Show*." Chuck Barris hosted that show. What about that other Chuck? Not Chuck Barry. Chuck Woolery. He hosted the *Love Connection*. He did "two and two." I wonder who came up with that. Did he? Was it a producer? Did he not know there was a number called "four"? That makes me start thinking about the number four. It's interesting that "four" is spelled f-o-u-r but "forty" is spelled f-o-r-t-y. Then of course I immediately think about building a couch fort. Maybe I should build a couch fort on the set of my show and have my guests talk to me inside the fort. That would be fun and entertaining and we should probably do it in our pajamas.

Once I realize that my mind has started to wander I stop and try to do what I'm supposed to do when that happens—focus on the third eye. Guess what? That makes me think about how great it would be to have a third eye. Would I want it on my forehead or on the back of my head? Maybe on the top of my head. No, 'cause of rain. What if my lips were eyes? Then

I'd get a lot more crumbs in my eyes, but I'd be able to get a really good look at what I'm eating. Just as I'm designing a pair of sunglasses in my head for my lip-eyes, the teacher hits the gong and I jump. I almost yell, "Oh my God!" but because I'm smart I yell, "Ohmmmmm!" I'm the only one chanting, but the class just thinks I'm really into meditation. The ohm actually calms me down so I leave feeling great. I'm peaceful, relaxed, and in a great mood. And now you see why it's so great to meditate.

Not to mention how much I think my memory has improved. It used to be terrible. I was never very good at remembering people—even people I had met before and even people who had been a guest on my show. I could spend an entire night at a fancy Hollywood party talking to someone and when Portia would ask, "Who did you talk to?" I would have to shrug and say, "It was either Marcia Cross or Zac Efron."

Now my memory is much, much better. I'll tell you more about that in a second. My phone's ringing. I'll be right back.

Meditation

Seriously...I'm Kidding

Ahhhhh. Doesn't that feel better?

Guided Meditation

Let's begin by getting in a comfortable position.

Sit or lie down and close your eyes.

Or if you're driving, keep your eyes open and fast forward through this chapter.

Now breathe in through your nose. Mmmmm. Doesn't that smell nice hopefully?

Now exhale through your mouth.

If you're on a crowded bus, apologize to the person whose face you just blew in.

Quietly say, "I'm sorry I just blew in your face."

And relax.

Feel your breath moving through your body.

We're inhaling energy. And we're exhaling stress.

Breathe in positivity and light. Breathe out negative thoughts like traffic...or flight delays...or bad service at a restaurant...or frustration with your boss...or a fight with your spouse or girlfriend or boyfriend...or money woes...or getting your car towed... or losing at Scrabble...or getting left at the altar...or finding out about a wheat allergy... or having one of your favorite socks stolen out of the dryer...or depression.

Don't dwell on any of those thoughts that I mentioned.

Say good-bye negative thoughts. We'll see you another time.

Now relax your mind.

You're in a meadow. A beautiful meadow with bright green blades of grass and no ticks.

It's peaceful and quiet. Listen to the wind blow across the meadow.

Do you hear it? That was an airplane. Listen closer. Listen to the leaves rustle and the snakes slither. No, not snakes. There are no snakes in this meadow. I shouldn't have said snakes.

Slow down your mind. Slower. Think about how slow you have to drive when there's someone on a bicycle in front of you in the middle of your lane. Are you annoyed? Don't be.

Today it's not annoying. Today it's peaceful.

Start to float above the meadow. Whoa. Look at that. You're floating. Are you scared of heights? Don't think about that.

Picture your wallet falling out of your pocket. You don't care. Let your wallet go.

A stranger picked it up, took the money out, and left the wallet behind. Let it go. You didn't need that money.

You're floating peacefully above the meadow.

As it turns out, there was a tick but it didn't bite you. So you're breathing out relief.

Feel the energy around you.

Now you're floating above water. There's a creek in the meadow. Or it might be a brook. You don't know the difference, maybe there isn't one. You don't care.

Just picture the creek-brook. Its winding

path piercing the meadow. The sun bouncing off the rocks. Don't think about how dangerous it would be to slip on them.

As you approach the water you see a bridge. It's a bridge that leads to happiness.

To the left of the bridge is a cape. Not a cape like a piece of land, an actual cape like a superhero would have. Put on the cape.

Now you have magical powers. You can do anything you want in this cape, except fly.

As you get closer you realize the whole bridge is made out of dark chocolate.

It's unsafe to walk on but so delicious to eat.

Carefully cross the bridge to happiness. Don't let anyone take your cape. It's yours.

People will try to take your cape out of jealousy, but don't let them.

On the other side of the bridge, they're showing classic reruns of *The Love Boat*.

Happiness is yours once you cross the dark chocolate bridge in your cape.

Be careful and good luck.

Random Things That
Might Help You
But Probably Won't

- Never make your bed with a monkey in it.
- Leaning forward in your chair when someone is trying to squeeze behind you isn't enough. You also have to move your chair.
- There's no attractive way to get a cherry pit out of your mouth.
- When making a right turn onto a busy street, always check the crosswalk for children's imaginary friends.
- Everyone looks better in fuchsia.
- If you have portraits of yourself up all over your house, people are going to

think you're conceited. Replace them with portraits of me.

- When moving heavy objects, I know they say to lift with your knees. I've always found it easier to lift with my arms.
- Rest rooms are not for resting.
- When your eye twitches, it means your body wants you to wink rapidly at whomever is sitting across from you.
- If you like winning, never play hide-and-seek with a chipmunk.
- Answering every question with "You got it, girlfriend!" can apparently be irritating to others.
- "Kerfuffle" is an actual word.
- At a four-way stop sign, the person with the prettiest eyes has the right of way.

American Idol, Or "If You Don't Have Anything Nice to Say, Don't Say Anything at All"

I have been a genuine fan of *American Idol* since it began. I love music. I love supporting new talent. And I love medleys about Ford. So it's always been one of my favorite shows. It turns out, however, I enjoy it a whole lot more when I get to watch from the comfort of my very own living room.

Everyone asks me about my time as a judge on *Idol*. People want to know what it's really like to be there, what Ryan is like, and what Simon is like. I'll say this about them: Ryan is truly a workaholic. He never stops. You don't see this watching from home, but during commercial breaks he goes around the audience selling Mary Kay cosmetics. And as for Simon—you can't always believe what you see. I know he comes across a certain way on TV, but in real life—and I don't mean to shock you—he's actually completely hairless.

When I first agreed to do the show, I thought it was going to be a lot of fun because, first of all, what great seats. You're right there in the front row. You're seeing everything live as it happens. You get unlimited refills of Vitaminwater. It seemed like a terrific idea.

But then reality set in and things changed. My schedule got crazy. Pressure started building. Randy kept calling me "dude." It was just very different from what I was originally expecting. I guess if I had to sum up my experience in one word, it would be "funfficult." It was really fun, but it was hard.

To give you a little sense of what my schedule was like during that year, I can walk you through a typical day. Normally, I tape my talk show at four o'clock every afternoon. I have all day to prepare and rehearse, and then from four to five I tape the show straight through.

A little secret about my show is that I tape it a day in advance of it airing on television. So when you're watching my show, let's say on a Wednesday, it's actually Tuesday for me. Your today is always my tomorrow and your yesterday is my today. Your last night is my tonight and your tomorrow is my two-days-from-now. But *American Idol* is always live. So I think you see what I'm saying. I never knew what day it was or where the hell I was.

To accommodate my schedule during *Idol*, we would tape my talk show at 2:30 instead of 4:00. That way we ended at 3:30 and I could jump in my car and drive across town to the *Idol* studios. It was always very stressful to get there on time since it's a live show, but luckily I'm pretty good at maneuvering through traffic. You just have to drive on the less-crowded streets. Well, not streets. Sidewalks.

Once I got to *Idol*, I would change out of my daytime talk show host outfit (casual chic), change into my prime-time outfit (judge's robe), and get prime-time hair and makeup (powdered wig, sex kitten eyes, etc.). Then I'd run onstage for the five o'clock show. Everyone there seemed to have a very busy schedule, and I assume that's why Simon never had time to button his shirt up all the way.

As hectic as my schedule was, the bottom line is that I don't like judging people and I don't like hurting people's feelings. That was the hardest part of being on that show for me. It was always easy for me to sit at home in my pajamas and critique performances, but when I was sitting at that judges' table ten feet away from kids who have put their heart and soul into the competition and they're staring at me hoping I'll say something nice and Simon's sitting next to me caressing my leg under the table, it was just difficult. I felt awful saying anything negative, so sometimes I would end up saying things like, "That was great" when really I wanted to say, "Uh-oh."

And I know there's such a thing as constructive criticism, but to me that's still criticism. It's just criticism with a jaunty hat. You're still hurting people's feelings, and I don't like it. I don't do it on my talk show. I don't do it in life. I just don't do it.

One of the reasons I didn't like giving criticism was that a lot of the contestants felt as if *Idol* was the end of the road. If they were eliminated, they thought it was all over. But that isn't the case. One of the good things about being there was that I got to tell them that there's a lot more waiting for them outside of *Idol*. In fact, the next day I had each contestant on my talk show, where I introduced them to a whole other audience, and I loved being able to do that.

It's the same with every career and life decision. You just have to keep driving down the road. It's going to bend and curve and you'll speed up and slow down, but the road keeps going. For me, I made a pit stop at *Idol*; it was exciting, and I'm grateful for the opportunity. But then I decided it was best for me to move on. So I got back in my hovercraft and I kept going down the road. Now I have my own record label and I can discover and nurture new talent, and that feels great.

And I'm still a huge fan of *Idol*. I watch it every single week. It's a great panel. Randy's been there from the very beginning. He's experienced and honest. There's the glamorous diva with the pretty hair and the jewelry and the gorgeous makeup. And then there's Jennifer Lopez, who doesn't look so bad herself. I love watching, and I'm happier now that I get to watch at home on my sofa with Portia and the only thing I have to judge is Portia's cooking. (That's just a joke! It's always delicious.)

Common Courtesy

I am never late. In fact, I'm usually early. This is partly because I believe in respecting other people's time, and partly because I forgot to turn my watch back after I went to Europe one summer. In a recent highly scientific study I conducted among friends, family, and cable repairmen, I discovered one thing to be true: Most people are always late.

I don't know when it became socially acceptable to be late. I imagine it started with the person who coined the phrase "fashionably late." What a terrible expression that is. I don't know who came up with it, but it was obviously someone smart enough to trick people into thinking that something is stylish when it is definitely not stylish. I'm assuming it's the same person who invented culottes.

I remember one time Portia and I invited a couple over for dinner and they showed up two hours late. You read that right—two hours! One hundred and twenty minutes. Seven thousand and two hundred seconds late. We told them to come at 7:00, and they got there at 9:00. By the time they showed up, we ran out of firewood for the fireplace, our candles had melted completely down, and I was capital D-runk. To be fair, I was drunk at 4:30, but that's not the point I'm making.

If someone invites me to a dinner party and they say to be there at 7:00, I'll show up at noon. And if they're not ready for me, I'll use that time to go through their medicine cabinets. I would never be late because it throws off the whole plan for the evening. Everyone schedules dinner parties the same way. You call it for 7:00. You expect people to trickle in between 7:00 and 7:15. There's about eighteen to twenty minutes of small talk, some appetizers, and by 7:45 it's time to eat. You eat for about an hour, drink a magnum or two of Chablis, have a heated discussion about politics and/or the quality of the *Look Who's Talking* sequel as compared to the original, and by 9:00 you're yawning so people know it's time to find their coats. When people don't show up until 9:00, everything gets pushed back far too late. By the time we were ready for dessert, I was ready for bed. Literally. I had put in my night guard and taken all my clothes off.

I understand that sometimes people are going to be late. I can deal with someone being ten minutes late or fifteen minutes late. But once you hit an hour, you better have a really good excuse—like, you gave birth to a baby in your car. And if you're gonna be more than an hour late, you better show up with a litter.

What I've realized is that people don't care about common courtesy anymore. How many times have you held a door open for someone who walks right through it without saying thank you? How many times have you let someone into your lane of traffic without receiving the courtesy wave? I mean, who among us hasn't picked up a drifter only to be disappointed after they steal all the money out of your wallet when you thought they were looking for gum? We've all been there.

And not only are people rude, they have no boundaries anymore. I was in a public ladies' room recently because the Port-O-Let that's usually part of my motorcade was in for repairs. And the person in the stall next to me was talking on her cell phone. In the stall. In public. Not a care in the world. On the one hand, I was happy for her because I found out her son made the honor roll and her husband got a promotion at work. On the other hand, I didn't need to know that her rash turned out to be nothing more than bicycle chafing.

When I was growing up, you couldn't take your phone anywhere because it was tethered to the wall in the kitchen. If you were on the phone, you were only on the phone because there was nothing else you could do except maybe flip through an old cookbook or rifle through a junk drawer full of pennies. You couldn't even bend down to tie your shoe or you'd get choked by six feet of phone cord.

Now that we can take our phones practically anywhere, everyone is completely distracted while they're supposed to be having a personal conversation. Have you ever been talking to someone and you can tell they're not paying attention to what you're saying at all? They pretend they are because every few seconds they say, "Uh-uh. Uh-huh. Oh really? That's so neat." And you're like, How is it neat that I have the flu?

It's crazy to me that people don't realize we can hear what's going on in the background of wherever they are. I know you're watching television because I can hear Anderson Cooper and I know he's not your roommate. I know you're in the grocery store because I can hear that grapes are on sale. I know you're at the gym because someone is telling you to feel the burn. At least I hope you're at the gym.

Everyone tries to multitask now and do twelve different things at once. I once saw a woman talking on the phone, putting on makeup, reading a newspaper, texting, and Twittering all at the same time. I went right over to her and said, "Hey! You need to focus right now. You are my therapist."

I guess what I'm saying is that politeness seems to be lacking in our society nowadays. In the 1950s people were much more polite. They used to say "G'day, ma'am" and "G'day, sir" and "G'day, mate." I might be thinking of the Australian outback. But still. People were polite. Wally and the Beav were never late for dinner. After Lassie rescued Timmy from the well, Timmy sent Lassie a handwritten thank-you note and a gift certificate to Denny's. And one of the biggest songs of the decade was called "Don't Be Cruel." Another one was "Be-Bop-A-Lula." (I don't know if that has anything to do with politeness, I just thought you might want to know.)

I'm not saying we should return to those times entirely. I mean, most ladies wore girdles and I don't think we need to revisit that situation. I'm just saying we can all work on our manners. We can say please and thank you.

We can be punctual. We can just be nicer to one another. It's something we have in our power to do. It reminds me of that Margaret Mead quote: "Never doubt that a small group of thoughtful, committed citizens can change the world. Indeed, it's the only thing that ever has." That's either Margaret Mead or it was my horoscope in last month's issue of *Yarn Today*. My point is, be nice and be on time.

Please.

Thank you.

Sauna

One of the best things you can do for your mind and body is sweat. That's why I usually wear undergarments made out of thick memory foam. It's also why I'm in a sauna right now. It's going to help me relax, rid my body of toxins, and clear my mind. Out with the old and in with the new!

It's very hot in here. I know I'm supposed to be sweating, but I don't know if I'm supposed to be sweating this much. There are little puddles of moisture collecting in the sleeves of my robe. I should probably take off my robe, but I'm just not that comfortable being naked around strangers. Unfortunately, the same cannot be said for most of the women at the spa today. It's like a nudist colony in here. I've never been to a nudist colony, but I imagine this is what they're like. A lot of naked people bending and stretching like they're preparing for a race.

Now my eyes are burning. Not because of the naked people. Well, a little because of the naked people. But mostly because of the heat. It must be about five hundred degrees in here. One time when I was a kid I stuck my head inside an oven because I wanted to get tan. This is much hotter than that. This feels more like the surface of the sun, or the inside of a jalapeño popper.

Saunas are supposed to be great for your skin. That's what my facialist's assistant's assistant told me. And I just learned on *Jeopardy!* that the skin is the largest organ in the human body. At first when Alex Trebek said, "This is the largest organ in the human body," I screamed out, "Leg!" Obviously I was just kidding. Well, I wasn't kidding but everyone laughed at me as soon as I said it so I pretended I was kidding. Sometimes I do that when I say something wrong and everyone laughs like I'm making a joke. They're always like, "Oh, Ellen, you're so funny." And I'm like, "Yep, gotcha again, you sillies!" And then I try to change the subject to Matt Lauer or something.

You know, I might be sitting too close to the heater. My eyelashes are sweating. I'm sure if I get some water I'll be okay. I love the cucumber water that spas have. It's so refreshing. It's like a little spa for your mouth. It's funny how cucumber water can taste so much better than pickle juice, even though it's from the exact same source. I love pickles, don't get me wrong. It's just that after a massage, I'd much prefer the lighter taste of cucumber water to the saltier taste of pickle juice. Whereas after a long day at the office, I might kick back in front of the TV and enjoy a large glass of pickle juice.

I don't know what I'm saying anymore. I would never have a glass of pickle juice. That's a lie. I think I'm delirious from the heat. The good news is, if I pass out at least I'm wearing a robe with a spandex bodysuit underneath it with a T-shirt and shorts over that. The bad new

Answers to Frequently Asked Questions

Yes.
Yes.
No.
One time in high school.
Three times in my twenties.
Rocks no salt.
Yes.
Four.
Never. And how dare you!
I will take no further questions.

Labels

Unfortunately, I get labeled a lot. I'm often labeled as a "gay talk show host" or a "vegan animal lover" or a "dancing superstar the likes of which this world has never seen before." I remember after I became a Cover-Girl, people started labeling me as just another "gorgeous blond model with a pretty face" and they stopped taking me seriously. And that was hard. That was really hard.

The problem with labels is that they lead to stereotypes and stereotypes lead to generalizations and generalizations lead to assumptions and assumptions lead back to stereotypes. It's a vicious cycle, and after you go around and around a bunch of times you end up believing that all vegans only eat cabbage and all gay people love musicals. (For the record, I find musicals very unrealistic. If I suddenly turned to Portia and burst into a song about how we're out of orange juice, I don't think she would just immediately join in. I think she would be confused and concerned for me.)

Stereotypes obviously come from somewhere. There are similarities among certain groups of people, but it would be dangerous to assume that all stereotypes are accurate. You can't say all New Yorkers are rude or all Californians are hippies. You can't say all blondes are dumb or all white men can't jump. You can't say all rich people are snobs or all celebrities have big egos and are self-centered. That's just not true.

But going back to me for a second. I know there are a lot of stereotypes associated with being gay. However, I didn't realize just how many there are until recently when a woman asked me how many cats I have. When I told her I have three, the first thing she said was "Oh, you really are a lesbian!"

And at first I thought, Well, yes I really am a lesbian. That secret's out. But then I thought, Wait, what? When did that become a stereotype? I thought most people who had a bunch of cats were single and lonely. No. See? That's another stereotype.

I was so taken aback by her comment. How does the number of cats you have make you a lesbian? And why is three the lesbian number? Would having only two cats mean I'm straight? Would having four make me a super-lesbian? I'd like to make it clear for anyone who may think otherwise, I assure you that having cats does not a lesbian make. There are a few other characteristics that define one as a lesbian.

When she said that, it reminded me of when I came out. At that time there were extreme groups that didn't think I was gay enough. There were other groups of people who thought I was too gay. It didn't occur to me that when I announced I was gay I would have to clarify just how gay I am. What does it matter? What does it mean? All I can say is I'm gay enough for me.

To me that's why stereotypes and labels can be so damaging. People make these sweeping generalizations and have preconceived notions of what you're supposed to be and of who you are based on a few tiny, little words. I think it's important to actually get to know someone before you make generalizations. And you can do that pretty easily just by talking to them, asking questions, or reading their diary.

Despite all the labels, in most ways I'm really not that different from anyone else. I guess if you had to label me, you could say I'm like the girl next door. Well, maybe not next door. I'm like the girl a few doors down.

For the Children—Part One

One of the things I love most about my talk show is the fact that everyone from babies to great-great-great-grandparents watches it. My show is fun for all ages, kind of like an amusement park or a strip club that offers day care.

Believe it or not, I have a loyal fan base made up of toddlers. I always assumed it was because they were impressed with my comedic timing and interviewing skills, but it turns out they just like to watch me dance.

I love that kids love my show. In fact, I love it so much I want to devote this chapter to them. On the next few pages you'll find pictures of cool things kids love that your son or daughter can color in. It's like a coloring book! Only better because it's my book! Please feel free to color it in yourself. You know that old saying: "You're never too old to play. You're only too old for low-rise jeans."

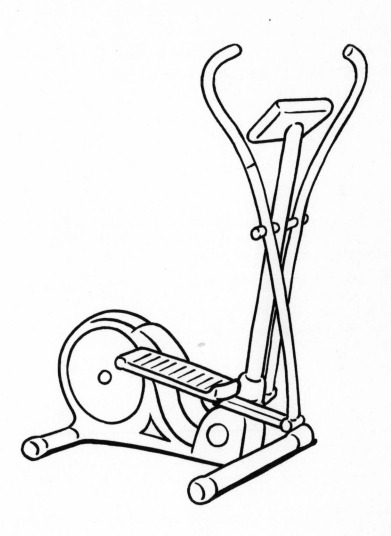

For the Children—Part Two

If there's one thing I know about children it's that they have a hard time understanding the meaning of the words "priceless Warhol."

If there's another thing I know it's that they love a good story. If it were up to them, kids would have you read them the same book five hundred times in a row. That can be very frustrating on the days you decide to read them *War and Peace.*

The real problem with kids wanting to hear the same story read over and over again is that as the reader, you get incredibly bored. So once again, Auntie Ellen is here to help. What I've done in this chapter is written a story that your child is going to want to hear many, many, many times. But the good news is, so will you! The parts of the story that are in parentheses are for adults, so as you read along be sure not to read any of that aloud.

Now get those kids into their pj's and let's get reading!

The Endlessly Exhilarating Adventures of a Pretty, Pretty Princess

BY ELLEN DEGENERES

Once upon a time in a land far, far away, there was a pretty, pretty princess named Isabella. She had long, flowing blond hair (most of it was a weave) and wore a tiara upon her head. She was often ridiculed for wearing her tiara because she never took it off—not when she ate breakfast or when she swam in the lagoon (or when she went out with strangers she met on Craigslist).

Many townspeople thought the king and queen had a peculiar daughter but the truth was Isabella didn't care what anyone thought of her.

She was a free spirit. (And she slept with a lot of older men.)

The king wanted Princess Isabella to marry a wealthy prince who lived in the next town over. But the princess didn't want to marry the prince because she wanted to explore the world before settling down, which in her mind meant she wanted to do a great deal of experimenting both sexually and with the illegal drug ecstasy—

Oh no, I'm so sorry. That was supposed to be in parentheses. I hope you didn't read that part aloud to your children. I'm so sorry!

The king and queen were both shocked that their daughter didn't want to marry the prince, for every young lady in all the land was envious of her opportunity. But Isabella meant it and so the king called off the wedding.

The princess was ecstatic. She immediately packed a bag and left for an exciting and magical trip around the world. (Her first stop was Amsterdam, where she immediately got a tattoo and started doing improv.)

She traveled all over every continent. (I think there are eleven?) One day she was walking through the beautiful streets of London when a sudden gust of wind blew her tiara right off her head. She ran into the street to get it just as a car was driving by. The driver slammed on his brakes so hard that everyone in the street stopped and stared.

Suddenly the driver stepped out of the car and Isabella couldn't believe her big, blue (fake contact lens–wearing) eyes. It was the prince.

Isabella couldn't explain why, but she was so happy to see him and he was happy to see her. He picked the tiara up off the street and placed it upon her head. (He had run it over with his car so it was in about four different pieces that he had to stack on top of one another.) He explained that he, too, wanted to spend time traveling and living on his own. But now as luck would have it, there they were together again. They embraced.

(They went back to their hometown and ended up getting married about a year later. Isabella gave birth to a bunch of kids throughout the next decade. She continued to wear her tiara outside of the house, which gave her the repu-tation of being a full-on weirdo, and she kept her hair long well into her late sixties. After the princess's father passed away, the queen moved in with them, which put some strain on their relationship. They got through it but there were definitely some rough patches. They had some money trouble on and off just like any other couple. A few of their kids weren't that smart. It seemed like they both couldn't help but wonder if they were meant to be together, even though it did seem like fate brought them back together that one day in London. Or maybe if she didn't wear that tiara all the time it wouldn't have blown off her head and they never would have seen each other again. It's one of those things that no one will ever really have the answer to.)

And they lived happily ever after. (Not really.)

Talking Hard

There are a few things I didn't realize would happen when I signed on to host my talk show. One, I didn't know that for the first three months of the job, I would have a recurring dream where Maury Povich invites me on his show to tell me that Phil Donahue is my biological father. And two, I didn't realize how much I was going to have to talk. Oh my heavens, there's a lot of talking. I know the job title is "talk show host," but I guess when I first started I focused more on the "host" part. I picked out nice candles for the guest dressing rooms. I made sure the lighting was just right. I stocked the rooms with champagne and fresh strawberries. I even picked out soft robes and underwear in case anyone wanted to get more comfortable. Sure, a lot of my guests initially thought I was hitting on them, and that was my mistake.

I just didn't realize how much talking it would involve, and my job isn't a job where I can ever take a day off. Believe me, I've tried. The studio is always like, "You signed a contract to be here every day, blah, blah, blah."

It's a lot of pressure. It turns out if I stop talking the show comes to a complete stop. It's the same as writing this book. If I don't write, nothing happens.

Do you see what I mean? It's pressure.

And it's not just the talking. I also have to listen! When I ask my guests questions, I don't know how they're going to answer so I really have to pay attention. In real life, when I ask someone a question I can nod and pretend like I'm listening, when really all I'm thinking about is how cute it would be if my cat could play the ukulele. If I daydream like that on my show, I'm being "rude" to "Julia Roberts."

Don't get me wrong—I love my job, but let me just break down how much talking there is on my show. Every day I start with a monologue. That's all talk with some occasional singing because when you have a voice like mine you have to share it with the world. Then I sit down and I talk to my DJ. We make small talk. After that I talk to my audience about what's going on in my life. I love talking to my audience. Over the past nine years, I feel like I've developed a relationship with them. It's one where I do most of the talking and we eat all our meals separately, but it works for us.

After I talk to the audience, we take a

commercial break, and during the break I talk to my producers. They tell me stuff like, "You look great" and "You were so funny when you said [INSERT HILARIOUS JOKE HERE]." It's not like they have to say that stuff or anything, but if they do they get entered into drawings to win fun prizes. Then we come back from commercial and I talk to my guests. Now, I love talking to my guests. I have had the chance to interview some absolutely incredible people—everyone from actors and musicians to powerful world leaders like the president of the United States and Justin Bieber.

But let me be clear. Not all of my guests are easy to talk to. Most of them are. Most of them come on with great stories to share and great energy. We have a nice time. We dance with each other, we chat, we do shots. But every once in a while, a guest will come on who isn't the easiest person to have a conversation with. I can't name any names, of course. Well, I can name one: Harry Connick Jr. He's like talking to a wall. It is impossible and I can't pretend otherwise anymore.

Meeting and talking to my guests is a

lot like being at a cocktail party with people you've only met once or twice. When you first see each other, you're not sure if you should shake hands or hug or kiss, so you end up doing that awkward handshake-half-hug-oh-my-goodness-we-almost-kissed-on-the-lips-because-I-didn't-know-which-way-to-turn-my-head! combination greeting.

Then after they sit down, I try to compliment them right away. I'll say something like, "You look great" or "It's so nice to finally meet you." And they'll say something like, "Thanks, you look great also" or "We've met before."

And then they'll launch into their personal stories.

I've definitely noticed some patterns over the years in the way certain people tell stories. First of all, you can always tell how interested you're going to be in a story based on how it starts. If it starts with the sentence "Wait until I tell you about my new shower caddy," I don't need to hear the rest of it. But if it starts "I survived twelve years in the jungle on nothing but berries and thistle," I'm in.

I've also noticed that when people say, "You

are never going to believe this story in a million years," I am almost always able to believe it. And when people say, "Long story short," they either say it after they've already told about fifteen minutes of an incredibly long, boring story, or they say it in the middle of what could be a really good story, like, "Well, we woke up and had breakfast out on the deck, like we do every morning. And long story short, I am no longer welcome in Mexico."

Obviously, it's my job to keep the conversation going and headed in a good, positive, upbeat direction. So I've learned that there are definitely questions to steer clear of to make sure that happens. If any of you ever decide to host your own talk show—and I encourage you to do so—here are some things you should never ask a guest:

1. How old are you really?
2. And where is *that* tattoo?
3. And where is *that* piercing?
4. What an interesting story that was about your belt. Tell me more.

5. Could we see more pictures of your
   wife giving birth in the tub?

I genuinely do love what I do. I like getting to meet new people every day, I like introducing my audiences to new music and talent, I like helping people. It's not like I'd rather be a mime. I mean, they have to wear far too much makeup.

Pros and Cons

By a show of hands, who has a hard time making decisions? You know what, I just realized I can't see you. This is a book! I wish I could see you. Well, not all of you. I don't know where you are or under what circumstances you're reading this. If you're sitting on a bench in a beautiful park, maybe somewhere in Colorado in the middle of summer, I'd love to be able to see you. Colorado is beautiful in the summer.

Or if you're sitting next to a fireplace, next to a big window overlooking a snowy field, maybe somewhere in Colorado in the middle of winter, I'd also love to be able to see you. Colorado is beautiful in the winter.

I'd love to be able to see some of you even if you're not in Colorado. It's just that a lot of people read books while they're in the bathtub and if that's the case, then I do not wish to see you. Unless you're in Colorado and it's fall and you have a breathtaking view of a lush forest from your bathtub. Then, perhaps.

Because I can't see you, I'll have to assume that a lot of you have a hard time making decisions. Sometimes I have a hard time making decisions and I like to think that I have a lot in common with my readers. (Who else considers a glass of wine a serving of fruit? Me, too!)

Throughout my career, I've had to make a lot of very big decisions, many of which had huge impacts on my life. The material I decided to do for my first appearance on *The Tonight Show* with Johnny Carson led to Johnny calling me over, which literally changed everything for me. (My decisions to sport a mullet with bangs and wear Hammer pants remain questionable.)

A lot of people are good at making decisions. They know what they want and they can make up their minds quickly. I call those people

"Quick Decision Makers." Some people, however, are very, very bad at making decisions. They waver back and forth and might linger on an issue for days or weeks or even years. I call those people "Annoying." Here's a fun fact: Quick Decision Makers are often stuck behind Annoying people in line at Starbucks.

Whenever I have to make an important decision, I like to make a list of pros and cons. That way I can see all the positives and negatives right there in front of me and I can decide what will work best for me. I highly recommend it. Can't decide if you should quit your big city job and move to a small town? Make a list. Not sure if you should plan a huge, fancy wedding or elope? Make a list. Debating whether to buy a really awesome fancy new car or send your kid to college? Make a list.

I wanted to show you how helpful a pros and cons list can be, so I've gone ahead and made a list of the pros and cons of making a list of pros and cons. Look it over and then you can decide for yourself if a list is right for you.

PROS

- Aids you in making well-informed decisions.

- Helps you to feel organized and in control of your life.

- Allows you to put off making an actual decision.

- You might decide to make your list while you're flying on an airplane next to a very attractive person. You'll take out a piece of paper and realize you need a pen. You'll ask him or her if he or she has a writing utensil, sparking a conversation about how you've both been to Paris in springtime. You'll fall in love, get married, and live happily ever after in a mansion made out of clouds.

- Lists are fun.

Pros and Cons of Making a List of Pros and Cons

CONS

- Forces you to make well-informed decisions so you can't say stuff like, "I don't know why I bought this ten-thousand-dollar antique spoon! I wasn't thinking."
- Takes away time that could be spent napping or playing video games.
- Takes away time from making your actual decision.
-   Can be hard to figure out margins.
- You might decide to make your list while you're flying on an airplane next to a very attractive person. You'll take out a piece of paper and rummage through your bag for a pen. Once you find it, you'll exclaim, "Found it!" and reach your arm up, immediately knocking it into the tray table of the attractive person next to you. Their water will go flying through the air, soaking them and you and the flight attendant, who happens to be walking by at the time. Everyone around you will be upset, you'll have to sit there without moving an inch for the rest of the six-hour flight, and you won't marry the stranger on the plane, something you've dreamed of doing since you were six.
- What was I trying to decide?

Additional Thank-Yous

I just remembered some people I forgot to thank in the acknowledgments. Deepak Chopra; my third-grade teacher, Mrs. Grady; the New Orleans Saints; my cats Charlie, George, and Chairman, who are my dawgs; my dogs Wolf and Mabel, who are really cool cats; everybody at NASA; Kate Middleton; and the nice man at the supermarket today who let me pay ahead of him because I only had one item. Thank you.

Babies, Animals, and Baby Animals

Peple are constantly asking Portia and me if we are going to have children. If you are one of the people or persons who want to know the answer to that question, before you stop me on the street or send me an e-mail or hand me back my dry cleaning, I can tell you right now that we are not going to have any children. We thought about it. We love children. We love to be around children after they've been fed and bathed. But we ultimately decided that we don't want children of our own. There is far too much glass in our house.

A few years ago in an online poll, Portia and I were voted the number one celebrity couple people would trust leaving their kids with. That's very flattering, but before anyone starts dropping their babies off at our house like it's a day care center, let me tell you how much I know about them. I know which end you feed. I know up from down. I know front from back on the boy ones. And I know that when they're born they're slimy and make weird goat noises. I might be thinking of a baby goat in that instance.

I know everyone says it, and that's because it's true—parents have the hardest job in the world. I can't think of anyone who has a harder job on the planet, besides maybe whoever glues those tiny rhinestones onto doll shoes. It's so precise.

Portia and I have learned so much about parenting from being around our niece Eva and her mom and dad. It's a challenge even if you have the most precious, most adorable, and cutest baby on the planet. (I know everyone says that about their own kids, and I'm sure you all think your kids are the cutest kids on the planet. It's sweet that you think that, but the fact of the matter is, Eva is the cutest.)

We've learned how much patience you need to have and how careful you have to be with what you say and what you do because from the moment these little creatures are born their brains are like sponges that absorb every single thing around them. We've also learned how attentive you have to be. If you're not attentive 100 percent of the time, you will quickly learn how difficult it is to get grape juice out of the antique rug in Auntie Ellen and Auntie Portia's sunroom.

Here's why I think every parent out there should be given a medal or a ribbon or a trophy, like those bowling trophies but instead of a person bowling on top there would be a little statue of a parent sitting down to watch some mindless TV after scraping dried peas off the sofa while their son or daughter is finally sound asleep in the other room. That might be too much to put on a trophy, but you get the idea.

First you have your baby, which in and of itself is a stunning feat. I won't go into specifics, but ouch and no thank you. Then you spend the next eighteen years raising the child.

Throughout that time you ask questions you have never before thought to ask another human being, like, "Who needs to go potty?" and "Can you please take your underwear off your head for Mommy?" and "You got what pierced? Where's that?"

Once your kids turn eighteen, you think you've done your job and you can go back to having a clean basement. But it turns out, according to an article I read, 80 percent of college graduates are now moving back home with their parents. Eighty percent! It would probably be 100 percent but some parents were smart enough to move without telling anyone.

That has to be frustrating for a parent. Your dream is to send your kid to college, be there when they graduate, and watch them go on to do great things. They're not supposed to come back home. Their room has already been turned into a gym.

That sort of thing doesn't happen in nature. When a bird leaves its nest, it leaves for good. The mama bird does all sorts of things to get those babies out of that nest for the long haul.

First she'll nudge them to encourage them to get up and move around. Then she'll show them how fun it is to fly. She'll circle the nest, swoop around, play peekaboo. Then she'll fly to another branch and squawk, "Hey, get out. I have company coming."

And the baby bird leaves. It learns to fly and make its own nest. It doesn't leave, get a bunch of tattoos, and come back to mooch off its mama. It starts looking for its own food and searching Craigslist for temp jobs.

I think parents can learn a lot about parenting from nature. Not only can they learn from birds, they can also learn from the wildebeest. When wildebeests are born, the parents encourage the babies to walk right away. And if they don't learn fast enough, they get eaten by a lion. So I guess what I'm saying is—parents, once those kids are out of college you've done your part. If they come back home after you've spent all that time and money on their college education, what you should do is get yourself a lion.

Okay, maybe don't get a lion. Maybe just change the locks.

Portia and I don't have any children. That's why we're always full of energy and smiling. But we do have a lot of animals that we treat like our family. We have two dogs, Mabel and Wolf, and three cats at home, Charlie, George, and Chairman. We have two cats on our farm, Tom and Little Sister, two horses, and two mini horses, Hannah and Tricky. We also have two cows, Holy and Madonna. And those are only the animals we let sleep in our bed.

We really treat our animals like they're our babies. We don't dress them up or anything. But we do take them to Mommy and Me classes every Friday. You should see the cows play the maracas during music time. If it isn't the most adorable thing you've ever seen.

I know having pets isn't exactly the same as having babies. It's not like I have to stay up all night nursing our cats. I mean, I do but I don't *have* to. But our animals have taught us valuable lessons that could be applied to parenting human babies, should we ever change our minds. Things like when your baby wants to communicate something, it will moo loudly.

And when your baby is hungry you will need to feed it some hay. Maybe that only applies to cows. But one thing we know for sure is that you should never sneak up on your baby, and when you're feeding it, you should always hold your hand flat. Now I'm thinking of a horse. You know what, we mostly know about animals. We're not gonna change our minds.

My Bucket List

1. Buy more buckets.
2. ~~Travel to distant lands to learn more about different people, cultures, societies.~~ Watch more Discovery Channel.
3. Wear more white.
4. Learn to fly.
5. Build a canoe.
6. Tell everyone I know I built a canoe.
7. ~~Go see the philharmonic, concerts, operas.~~ Watch more PBS.
8. Call more people "rascal."
9. Watch someone run a marathon.
10. Learn to speak a foreign language, like Australian or British.

I Am Not Lazy

I am not a lazy person. In fact, I'm a very busy, hardworking person. I host a daily talk show. I have my own production company. I have my own music label. On the weekends I manage a Kinko's downtown. But every once in a while I do something very lazy, shockingly lazy.

A few months ago, I got home from a long day of entertaining America and many other parts of the world and I sat on my sofa to watch some television. I realized my favorite cat, Charlie, wasn't with me. She usually finds me as soon as I come home. My other cats are more independent. They spend summers backpacking through Europe and call when they need me to wire money.

But Charlie and I have a very special relationship and I wanted to let her know I was home. Don't worry, I'm not one of those crazy cat ladies. I just like my favorite cat to know I'm home so we can talk, have dinner together, and watch *Hoarders*.

I assumed she was in our master bathroom because that's where the cats like to hang out when we're not home. They record most of their "cute kitty plays with loofah" YouTube videos in there.

Now, in order to let her know I was home I could have walked to the bathroom or yelled for her, which is what I usually do. But for some reason on that day I did something else. We have an intercom where I can push a button and talk to someone in another room. Sometimes it's fun to use when we have company. I'll get on it from a different part of the house and whisper stuff like, "Is there anything you ever really wanted to tell God? I'm listening." Oh, we have fun.

Anyway, I got on the intercom and I said, "Charlie, I'm home! Charlie!" and I hung up and I waited for Charlie to come running. I didn't think anything of it until I looked over and Portia was staring at me.

She said, "Did you just intercom the cat?"

And I looked at her and I had no choice but to say, "Yes. I did just intercom the cat."

In my defense, I was very tired and if I wanted to walk all the way to the bathroom to find Charlie I would have had to get on my Segway, ride it to the escalator, take the escalator to the third floor, cross the champagne fountain, get my retina scanned, and deactivate dozens of laser beams.

Okay, that isn't true. I would have had to walk down the hall.

I'm not usually that lazy. Have I ever tried to take my pants off without taking my shoes off first? Yes. I also recently got in my car one morning, noticed a stain on my shirt, and then continued to drive to work instead of going all the way inside to change.

I'm sure you have all done that at some point. You get dressed in the morning and you're excited about your outfit. Right before you leave the house, you notice a coffee stain right in the middle on your shirt or a little hole right in the armpit. Of course that means you put it back in your closet like that after you wore it the last time. "Oh, that's not too bad. I can wear that again."

Once you see it, instead of having to go back and find a new shirt to match the pants and shoes and neckerchief you already picked out, you shrug and say, "I'll just tell people it happened on my way to work."

We're getting lazier and lazier. There is so much technology that helps us be lazy. There are now cars that park themselves, which is great not only for lazy people but for people who also hate not having scratches on their bumpers. There are vacuums that vacuum for us. Thanks to Bud Light Lime, we don't even need to squeeze the lime into our own beer anymore.

Humans aren't supposed to be so lazy. We're not supposed to go from work where we sit for hours and hours in the same chair staring at the same computer screen to our homes where we spend hours and hours sitting on our sofas playing video games and watching reality TV.

I'll admit I'm guilty of watching a lot of reality TV. Nothing makes me feel lazier than complaining I can't find the TV remote to change the channel—and then eventually finding it so I can watch an episode of *I Shouldn't Be Alive* about a sailor who had to float on a twig in the middle of the ocean for two months after his boat capsized and sank.

It wouldn't be so bad to watch all these reality shows if they weren't so time consuming. They're each two hours long! There's a dent in my couch the shape of my entire body and it got there after I watched a single episode of *The Bachelor*. I also like to watch *American Idol*, *Survivor*, *The Celebrity Apprentice*. That's like ninety-seven hours of TV to watch every week. That barely leaves any time to focus on what's truly important in life—Facebook and Twitter.

By the way, I've noticed that there is a show to find the "next" everything—the next model, the next chef, the next designer, singer, dancer, entrepreneur. Pretty soon there will be a reality show to pick the next president. We won't even have to leave the house to vote. "Sorry, sir, during this debate you did not stuff enough marshmallows into your mouth. You will not be moving on to the primaries. Please bring me your torch."

What they should do to save us all some time is combine every show into one giant reality show. Who wouldn't watch a show about the next tap-dancing celebrity bachelor apprentice who can survive in the wilderness while singing about losing weight? Ryan Seacrest would host and we would all watch.

Let's all challenge ourselves today to get up and move a little more. You know what we should be doing more of? Squatting. Let's all squat more. For every YouTube video you watch, do a squat. For every video game you play, do a lunge—not at someone. Then squat again. And then thrust. And then lunge again. And then squat. And then thrust.

And now work your arms by turning the page. You're doing a great job.

Note: This chapter was dictated but not read.

Aspirations: A Short Short Story

"I want to be an astronaut when I grow up," said young Delilah.

"You live in a tiny village outside a small town next to a great big city," said her mother. "You will stay here and work on our farm. You will never be an astronaut."

Indeed, Delilah worked on the farm for many years and grew old. On her final day, in the care of local villagers, she turned and asked, "Was I an astronaut?" And they said, "Yes. You were a great astronaut." And she said, "Really? I was?" And they said, "Shhhh. No more talking."

Social Skills

There has never been a time when people could communicate and express themselves as instantly and as much as they can now. It's hard to believe, but there was a time when communicating meant we had to WRITE LETTERS! (If you're reading this book to your kids as a bedtime story, and I highly suggest you do, now might be a good time to teach them about handwritten letters, record players, VCRs, and the first season of *The Hills*.)

Nobody writes letters anymore, which means nobody has pen pals. I remember when I was probably about ten years old I had a pen pal, and writing letters back and forth with him was one of my favorite things to do. His name was Steve and he lived in one of those huge mansions that's so big it has a name. It was called the Louisiana State Penitentiary, and he told me it was even bigger than the mayor's mansion. We'd send letters back and forth and he'd ask me to send him my favorite books and small pieces of metal or wood that were lying around and all the money I could find in my house. And I'd gather them all up and put cute little stickers of cats on the packages and send them away. It was so fun. Eventually we stopped writing because I moved to another city and he moved out to live on his own. He called it "solitary confinement." I was always so impressed by his vocabulary.

I've always liked writing. I like the feeling of having a nice pen in my hand. It feels like I'm creating something when I put pen to paper, even if it is just a doodle of a flower or a note that says, "If you ever park in my spot again I will have your ass towed." It's a nice feeling.

When you physically write something down you're forced to take time to actually think about what you're writing. We don't really do that anymore. Now we just press buttons. We can delete things and change things at our leisure. We're so spoiled. Think about what cavemen had to go through when they wanted to write something down. They had to chisel it into stone. It probably took hours just to write "Dear Krog. Going out for bread. Be back in twenty. Glok." If they made a mistake they'd have to go out and find another flat stone and start all over. Who knows if they ever even made it out for bread. I do know they used to club each other over the head a lot, so I'm not saying we should do everything like the cavemen. I'm just saying nobody writes letters anymore.

Now everything is electronic and instantaneous. We e-mail, we text, we Facebook, we Twitter, Skype, instant message, iChat, blog, dance interpretively on YouTube. Every person who has a passing thought, opinion, question, or answer can express it immediately on his or her computer, phone, laptop, tablet, or other portable electronic device that will be invented and revolutionize communication in the short window of time between my writing this book and it being published.

Way, way back in the day, like in the 1990s, if you wanted to tell everyone you ate waffles for breakfast, you couldn't just go on the Internet and tweet it out. There was only one way to do it. You had to go outside and scream at the top of your lungs, "I ate waffles for breakfast!" That's why so many people ended up in institutions. They seemed crazy, but when you think about it, they were just ahead of their time.

Right this second, someone is probably reading this book and thinking, "I'm thirsty for tequila." I'm guessing that's what they're thinking because that's what I'm thinking as I write it. So that reader is going to take to their Twitter account and tweet, "Reading Ellen's hilarious new book. Thirsty for tequila." And if that makes people want to buy the book, I think that's great.

What's not so great is that all this technology is destroying our social skills. Not only have we given up on writing letters to each other, we barely even talk to each other. People have become so accustomed to texting that they're actually startled when the phone rings. It's like we suddenly all have Batphones. If it rings, there must be danger.

Now we answer, "What happened? Is someone tied up in the old sawmill?"

"No, it's Becky. I just called to say hi."

"Well, you scared me half to death. You can't just pick up the phone and try to talk to me like that. Don't the tips of your fingers work?"

It's even more awkward when we're face to face with people. It used to be exciting to make plans with friends because you could sit and catch up and talk about what's been going on in your lives. Now when you see someone there's nothing left to say. You've already seen the pictures from their trip to Rio on Facebook. You've read their tweets about the latest diet they're on. And they already texted you about the pregnancy scare. So you end up just sitting and staring at each other until you both start texting other people.

Whatever we do say has to be short because

our attention spans are now about nine seconds long. We talk in short bursts. We can only read up to 140 characters at any given time before we're on to the next thing. We don't even have the patience to wait for Minute Rice. We've moved on to instant rice. Because really, who has time to wait a full sixty seconds for rice? I'll tell you who. Nobody.

We have TiVo because we don't have the time or patience to sit through commercials. And we have on demand because we don't just want movies and TV shows available to us at any given moment, we downright demand it.

Just to give you a little example of how patient people used to be, did you know that the opening credit sequence to *Mister Ed* back in the early sixties was a solid minute long? (I'll give you thirty seconds to pull it up on your phone so you can see it for yourself.) People had no choice but to sit through the whole thing, and they loved it. They paid attention to it. "A horse is a horse, of course of course. And no one can talk to a horse of course. That is of course unless the horse is the famous Mister

Ed!" And it keeps going, for almost a minute more. Now the opening theme song to a TV show is a guitar sting. "Ba-bow!" And we're inside someone's kitchen.

Now granted there wasn't anything else for people to watch on TV at that time so they didn't have much of a choice. It was either sit through the theme song or play with a yo-yo.

I bet a lot more people read back then. I have to say it's impressive that you're taking the time right now to read this book. It's so rare for people to actually set aside time to curl up with a book and read. By the way, I don't know why you have to curl up to read a book, but that's what people say. You can't just say you're going to read a book because then someone will ask, "Well how are you gonna read it? What position will you be in?"

"I'm gonna curl up."

"Oh, good. So you're not gonna stand?"

"No, no. I'm gonna curl up."

"Okay, good. Hey, you're not gonna lay on your side, are you?"

"No. I promise. I'm just gonna curl up."

It's an awkward position to be curled up. I like to lie flat or try out a lot of different positions—I'm still talking about reading. We don't curl up to do other things. We never say we're gonna curl up and surf the Internet or curl up and knit. In fact, if you're curling up while you're doing anything besides reading you might want to look into Boniva.

Anyway, what was I saying? Oh yeah, we lose focus, have no attention span, yada, yada, blah, blah, blah. You know what—you can check out my Twitter page or go to my website for more information on this.

Dinner with a Psychic

A friend of mine recently told me she went to a dinner party with a psychic. It really struck me as a fascinating concept. It's one thing to go to a psychic and have a consultation, but it seems like a whole other thing to socialize with one. Could he read her mind the whole time? Did he know when the party was going to get boring? Did he know when they were going to run out of bean dip?

Here is how I imagine the conversation went at dinner between my friend and the psychic. In this dramatic interpretation I will refer to my friend as "Susie" and the psychic as "Psychic."

SUSIE: Hi, I'm Susie.

PSYCHIC: I know.

SUSIE: How do you know Janet?

PSYCHIC: I knew you were gonna ask me
that. We met through mutual friends.
How do you know Janet?

SUSIE: We went—

PSYCHIC: Just kidding. I already know.
Do you want me to pass you the salad?

SUSIE: Yes, please.

PSYCHIC: I knew you did. Would you like
more water?

SUSIE: No thanks.

PSYCHIC: I knew you didn't.

SUSIE: Okay, well it was really nice talking
to you.

PSYCHIC: You're going to have spinach in
your teeth later.

SUSIE: Thanks.

PSYCHIC: I knew you were gonna say that.

Ideas

There's a famous quote—"When genius strikes one must be ready to play, or they shall be at the mercy of the taskmaster." I don't know if you're familiar with it or not. Okay, I just made it up.

But while I was writing this book, a lot of my ideas came to me at all sorts of crazy times—out at dinner, in the middle of the night, even while hanging upside down on a Pilates machine. I never knew when a brilliant idea was going to hit me because my brain is working 26/7. Since I wanted to be prepared at all times, for the past year I kept a pen and paper on my person—don't worry about the specifics of where or how. And every time I had a great idea, I would write it down so I wouldn't forget it.

Here's an idea that came to me while I was hanging upside down on my Pilates machine eating dinner in the middle of the night. I think it will prove to you that genius can strike at any moment of any day.

Do you ever notice how people— Hang on, I can't make out that word. I think it says "smile." Does that say "smile"? No. Maybe it says "simile." Why would I write down the word "simile"? I don't even use that word in my daily life. Why would I write it down? Is that a "Q"? Or a "G"? I don't know what that says. Does it say "monkey"? I don't remember thinking about monkeys. I remember thinking about pineapple, but that does not look like pineapple. Actually, it kind of looks like *a* pineapple. It just doesn't look like the word "pineapple." Maybe it says "Greenland." I was just thinking about Greenland. Or was it Iceland? Where does Björk not live? Is this even my handwriting? Who wrote this? Is that blood? No, blood isn't light blue. It's definitely ink. What is that word? Astronaut milkshake?

I'm sorry, maybe I shouldn't have written this chapter.

For the Teenagers

This chapter is 4 cool kids only. U NO WHO U R.

OMG. I'm so happy ur reading this bk. I no I don't no u, but u r so cool. LOL.

Just want 2 say hi and how r u. What r u doin 2 nite? I M going out l8r 4 dinr w/frenz. I hope they r on time or I will b ☹.

Here's a fun-e stor-e. 1 time I told my bro LYLAS. He wuz like whaaaa? And I wuz like J/K! LYLAB. It wuz 2 funny. He wuz like u r 2 much LN. 2 much. LMAO.

N E way...do u like U2? I <3 U2. Do U 2 <3 U2? GJKLE#*OJPOK,LVORPA//%$#. Ooops,

I fell asleep on my keyboard!!!!!! OMG!
ROTFL.

OK, g2g. TY 4 reading. KIT. ☺. TTYL. C U
L8R. FSBO.

<3, E

For the Adults Who Don't Understand the For the Teenagers Chapter and Really Want To

This chapter is for the cool kids only. You know who you are.

Oh my God. I'm so happy that you are reading this book. I know I don't know you, but I can tell that you are so cool. Just thinking about the fact that I don't know you, but can still tell that you are cool makes me want to laugh out loud for some reason.

Well, I just want to say hi and see how you are doing. Hey, what are you doing tonight? I am going out later for dinner with a few friends. I hope they are on time or I will be very, very sad.

Here's a funny story that I think you'll enjoy. I remember there was this one time I was talking to my brother and I said, "I love you like a sister." And he looked at me incredulously and said, "What?!" And so then I said, "Just kidding! I love you like a brother." It was too funny. He was like, "You are too much, Ellen! Too much!" Just thinking about it again right now is making me laugh so much that I am actually laughing my ass off. That's how funny it is to me. I am laughing my ass off. Bye-bye, ass!

Anyway, do you like the band U2? I love U2. Do you like them also, the band U2, that is? GJKLE#*OJPOK, LVORPA//%$#. Ooops, I fell asleep on my keyboard!!!!!! Oh my God! I can't believe I did that!

That is funny. That is actually so funny to me that I am currently rolling on the floor laughing. Previously, my ass was falling off from laughing so hard. Now I cannot help but roll around on the floor because of how funny that is.

Okay, I got up off the floor and now I have to get going. Thank you for reading this chapter. Please keep in touch. I am so happy right now. I will talk to you later. Who knows? Maybe I'll even see you later. For sale by owner.

Love, Ellen

The Longest Chapter

You might be able to tell from its name, but I just want to make it clear up front that this chapter is the longest chapter in this book. So if you are planning on reading one more chapter before you go to bed or squeezing in one last chapter before you leave for dinner, this might not be the chapter for you to read right now. Because it's long. Very, very long.

If you'd like, I can tell you really quickly what it's about and why it's so long and then you can decide whether or not you want to keep reading it now or come back to it later. And trust me, I will not be offended if you decide to come back to it. I'm not that easily offended.

Maybe if you said you didn't like my shirt or my shoes my feelings would be a little hurt, but otherwise I like to think I'm pretty tough. Plus, I'm the one giving you the option to either keep reading or skip it for now, so it would be weird if I was like, "Hey, why didn't you keep reading instead of going to your doctor's appointment? My feelings are hurt!" Because I'm giving you the option.

In fact, for your convenience I've made the next chapter of the book a short one. So you might want to skip ahead to that chapter and make that the last one you read before you put the book down, and then you can come back to this chapter later. Just don't forget to come back to it! Maybe you want to dog-ear this page or bookmark it or write a note to yourself so you remember to read it. I know folding the corner of a page ruins the aesthetic of the book and you might lose money should you ever try to resell it, but that's what makes life so difficult. It's the choices you make.

The reason this chapter is so long is because it's the most compelling chapter in the whole book. I'm going to tell you about something that changed my life forever.

That probably makes you want to keep reading! I don't mean to try and tempt you to stay. I would feel really awful if I made you late for a date with someone who could have been your future spouse were it not for your unattractive quality of being tardy.

It's just that I know people want to hear compelling things about me that I've never shared before. When I first started writing this book, people kept asking me, "What's in this book that I'm not going to hear anywhere else? Why should I read it? What's so special about it?" And I would always answer the same way. "Why don't you just buy the book because you love me, Mother?"

But I understand what people are saying. I know I'm on TV every day talking about my life. You can read about me online or in magazines. I have that blog about flowers that has over eighty subscribers. Y'all know a lot about me. But you don't know everything, and that's what this chapter is about.

And I certainly don't mean to make this chapter even longer by talking about how long it is. It almost feels like I'm making you wait and wait and wait and I'm never going to get to my point, and I assure you that's not the case.

But then again, maybe that's the lesson here. Maybe we all need to slow down and stop running from one place to another all the time. Maybe whatever you're about to do can wait. Sometimes waiting can be really good for you. As an example, it's always a good idea to wait at least a half hour after you've eaten before you go swimming. Some people say that's a myth, but I say better to be safe than sorry. I wait a half hour after eating before I go anywhere near water, and that includes swimming, bathing, showering, and panning for gold.

Obviously, there are some times when waiting isn't great. Waiting on hold on the phone can be annoying. Waiting for the results of an exam or on something like a pregnancy test can be very stressful, I would imagine. And what about how frustrating it is when you have to wait in line for the ladies' room? What takes so long in there, you guys?!

But at the same time, if you're waiting for something good like a new movie to come out or for your family to leave town, there's a feeling of anticipation that can be very exciting. There's suspense and drama as adrenaline starts to rush through your body like a rocket or like the water that shoots down through those dirty waterslides at theme parks.

Right now you're probably wild with anticipation. "What is she gonna say? What's her story? I can barely wait another second to hear something she's never told anyone!"

And by the way, thank you so much for waiting and reading this chapter all the way through. I have to say I would find it rude if you decided to skip ahead or put the book down after I explicitly stated that I was going to share something for the very first time that changed my life.

It's not like it's the only thing I'm sharing in this book that I've never told anyone. There's actually a lot in here that I've never shared before. I would say that nearly every single page has a new thought or a new idea or a new word that I've never before uttered. Here's one right now. Quoth. I've never said that word before. I've never talked about it. This is the only place I will ever mention or discuss the word "quoth."

Here's another thing: I'm allergic to penicillin. Bet you didn't know that, did you? That's because I've never told anyone that. Not even a doctor.

Here's another thing I've never talked about: I think it's weird that all dance classes have to be taught in front of a huge glass window. It's the only business that leaves nothing to the imagination. Why no curtains? Why do they want people walking by and staring at them? I have nothing against leotards, but that's a lot of bits and pieces for my eyes to see when I'm just trying to get to the coffee shop next door.

Anyway, those are all things that I've never shared with anyone ever before and as purchasers of this book I hope you feel special that you are the only ones to have this information. Those aren't even part of what I set out to share with you in this chapter. Those are just bonus ideas.

What I really wanted to tell you is what seriously changed my life forever. I've never been the same since I first laid eyes on it and it's one of the best things that has ever happened to me.

It's the Swiffer.

You know what? That's it. I honestly thought it was going to take more time to explain how it changed my life, but I think you get it with that one word.

I guess this chapter isn't the longest chapter after all.

Tweet Chapter

An observation in 140 characters.

How come when you wipe up dust it's called dusting but when you wipe up a spill it's not called spilling? There's something to think about.

Deep Thinkers and Not So Deep Thinkers

You're probably familiar with the famous sculpture of *The Thinker*. It's a man sitting down with his head resting on his hand, and it was created by a French artist named Rodin in 1902. It represents a person deep in thought, contemplating the struggles and the heaviness of the world around him. I recently saw a replica of it in the garden department of Sears and it got me thinking.

There are obviously all different sorts of people in this world. That's what makes the world go 'round. Well, that and wind. But when I saw *The Thinker*, I started to really think about thinking and I thought about this: There are two distinct types of people in the world—deep thinkers and not so deep thinkers.

Deep thinkers are people who ask a lot of questions, who are conscious about their actions, who seek reasons and explanations for everything they do and see and hear. Not so deep thinkers are people who litter. They're less aware of their impact on the planet. I mean, what year are you living in if you think you can still roll down your car window and toss garbage into the street? Maybe that was super awesome in 1968 but we can't do that anymore. It's not cool, man.

We all need to be deeper thinkers. We need to think more about our actions and their consequences. There's a law of physics that says "For every action there is an equal and opposite reaction." Do you know what that means? Me neither. Actually, it might have been in my fortune cookie last night. My point is, we need to think about what we are doing on and to this planet. We only have one Earth and it's the most important planet in our entire solar system, besides Uranus.

The more we consciously think about what we're doing and what we're consuming, the better off we're going to be. And I don't just mean what we eat. I mean what we buy and what we use. We consume so much. We buy the latest computers and phones and TVs and clothing, and that means everything that came before it ends up in landfills and oceans. I know that's not a particularly hilarious sentiment but it's something we need to think about as humans. And if you're an alien living on Earth, you should be thinking about it as well. Everyone should think about it—not just the people who get labeled "hippies" or "tree-huggers" because they care about our environment. I care and I'm not a hippy. I did hug a tree one time, but it was the seventies and I thought the tree was my friend Judy.

There's plenty we can do to help. First of all, if you're not recycling I don't even know what to do with you right now. I hate to have to scream at you through this book, but PLEASE RECYCLE!

Secondly, there's a very easy way to save water.

Take group showers. It's fun. It's friendly. At first, my housekeepers were resistant to this idea, but luckily my landscaper talked them into it.

Another thing you can do is take reusable bags to the grocery store. Now I always thought a reusable bag that you bring into a store was called a purse, and from what I understand putting things in your purse while you're shopping is called shoplifting. So, shoplift.

Want to save electricity? Unplug your appliances when you're not using them. Every Sunday, I unplug my tanning beds and dim the lights in my discotheque. You might want to unplug your television for a few hours a day. Not while my show is on of course, but any other time. Well, not if it's Shark Week because that's fascinating programming, but any other time. Unless *The Bachelor* is on because people are going to be talking about it at work the next day. And if *So You Think You Can Dance* is on you gotta watch that. You know what, never mind. Don't unplug the TV. Get rid of your refrigerator or something. I don't know. You'll figure it out.

We all know people who go through life without ever thinking about their actions. They're the people who don't use turn signals and choose not to replace the empty roll of toilet paper after they finish it. They're not malicious in their intentions (usually). They just aren't paying attention.

Let's try and pay more attention to what's around us. Look up. Look down—if only so you don't trip. Ask questions. You know how kids always ask "why?" Ask why. Then ask why again. And then ask why again. And then ask why again. And then ask why again. And then ask why again. And then ask why again. And then ask why again. Don't stop asking why until you get the answer you're looking for. Or until you're escorted away by security, whichever comes first.

Here's a question: If our Earth is turning at one thousand miles per hour, why can't I jump on a trampoline in Los Angeles and end up at a diner in Phoenix a few minutes later? Right? Think deeply about that for a while.

Chapter for the Audiobook Listeners

I know many of you are listening to an audio version of this book, so I'd like to say a special hello to all of you. Recording an audio book is a lot like doing the voice of an animated character in a movie. I'm in a recording booth and I have big headphones on and I'm talking into a big microphone. And since there are no cameras I don't have to wear any pants.

There is a sound engineer. Hi, Jerry! I'm waving to him right now. He's sweet. He's waving back. Hi! Now he's holding up a sign. "My name isn't Jerry. It's Mike."

Anyway, since you have the benefit of being able to hear this, I thought I would include some bonus material of me making strange noises.

For those of you who are reading this the old-fashioned way and can't hear me, I've printed the noises below and I encourage you to use your imagination to think of what they might sound like coming out of my mouth.

Meeeeee
Faaaaa
Cooooooooooo
Gooooooood morning
Bowwwwwww
Babowwwww
Yellowwwww
Kentucky!
Pop
Pop pop pop
Kerplunk
Lemonade
Sylvia
Click
Pah-pah-pah-pah-pah-pah-pah-pah-pah-pah-pah
Pew pew pew pew pew pew pew
Shhhhhhhh
Harumph!

Honesty

They say honesty is the best policy. But is it? It is. Actually, honesty is one of the qualities I find most attractive in a person. (Another one is nice ankles.)

Honesty is so important and yet a lot of times it's hard to find in people. I'm not saying any of you are liars. I don't know you. I'm sure you're sweet and nice and have never "accidentally" dropped a jury summons down a garbage disposal. Maybe you've never uttered so much as a fib in your whole entire lives. But let's face it, you probably have. We all have. Well, I haven't. I'm always honest.

Okay, see? That was a lie. And I'm sorry.

We might not go around spewing huge, sweeping, outrageous lies, but in one way or another most of us lie every now and again. I actually read a statistic that on average people lie four times a day. I don't know exactly what four lies people are telling each day but I do know that people tend to lie about their age, their weight, their natural hair color, and how cute their friends' babies are. "What a cutie-pie. Look at those ears! You have to—can't miss 'em! So cute."

I also know that people lie on their résumés. People lie under oath. People lie to their doctors, which I've never quite understood. I know you might be embarrassed about how you got that bite on that particular part of your body, but you have to be honest about it so a trained professional can help you.

I really try my best not to lie. That's true. I try to give my honest opinion on things. I try to tell it like it is. Give it to 'em straight. Lay it on the line. Be up-front. Keep it real. Not say false…stuff. I don't know any other sayings. I try not to lie.

Sometimes it's hard because I don't like to hurt people's feelings. So there have been times when a friend will get a haircut and I will see it and my initial reaction is "Oh my God, you look like a streetwalker who got caught in a wind tunnel." But I obviously can't say that because that would be an insult to streetwalkers. So I have to say, "I love it! It looks great!" But when I say it my voice goes up about three octaves. "It looks greee-aaattt!" So I'm certain they know I'm lying.

How come when we lie our voices go up so many octaves? It's a dead giveaway. It happens when we dole out compliments we don't mean and it happens when we say things like "You didn't have to get me anything!" or "What do you mean you weren't invited to my party? You're always invited!" Everyone knows what those mean. "You definitely had to get me something" and "You haven't been invited back to the house since the urn incident of '04." And it's a mathematical fact: the higher the octave, the bigger the lie. "I didn't even hear my phone ring!" is usually like a four on the scale. "You think I'm sleeping with someone else?!" is off the charts.

I can tell when people are lying to me when they start their sentence with "I have to be honest with you." They may as well say, "Listen, I'm about to lie straight to your face." Why do people need to clarify when they're being honest? Does that mean everything else they've ever said has been a lie? Yesterday they said they liked my sweater but they didn't say they were being honest. Does that mean they hated it?

It's so strange to me. It almost feels like they're giving me the option to not hear the truth. As if when they say, "I have to be honest with you," I might say, "No, no. Please. Only lies right now."

For the most part, we're honest people. Which is good because when you think about it everything around us is based on the honor system. Look at airport baggage claim. We all stand around a conveyor belt totally unsupervised and all those bags are there for anyone to take. I know because I was at the airport recently and I took four. I got some good stuff— three travel irons and a large man's nightshirt.

There are a lot of places that rely on us to be honest. Banks put out candy and hope you only take one or two pieces. Restaurants put out toothpicks. Libraries have those giant statues of lions out front. They're practically begging us to get a crane and a flatbed truck to cart those things away.

Think of how honest we're expected to be when we go to the movies. We pay for one ticket but in theory we can sneak into as many theaters as we want once we're inside. We can even pay the child's price and sneak in our own popcorn and vegan appetizers. I'm guessing.

And as much as certain people and places rely on us to be honest, we rely on others to be honest with us. I mean, we hand our car keys over to a complete stranger at the valet just because he's wearing a vest. (By the way, now you now why I wear a lot of vests and have so many cars.)

It's nice to think we can trust each other. It would be depressing to walk around every day thinking people are lying to us all the time. I prefer to believe people are good and honest and respect me enough to tell me the truth. It's not easy to find those people all the time, but they're out there. They're usually the people who don't hesitate to tell you when you look tired or that you have broccoli hanging from your lip. They might be blunt and sometimes they might hurt your feelings with their candor, but honestly? You'll appreciate it.

Don't Worry, Be Happy

If there is any message I want you to take from this book, it is that befriending a parrot can be both frustrating and infinitely rewarding. And if there is another message I want you to take from this book, it's that you can be happy. There is so much bad news in the world right now and sometimes it's hard to see the positive side of things, but it is possible and there are things you can do to be happy.

In the interest of full disclosure I want you to know that I'm not a spiritual adviser. Yes, it's true that if my mother didn't name me Ellen she was going to name me Deepak. But she didn't and that is not the path I followed. And

I would never want to mislead you by telling you that I have all the answers, because I don't. I mean, I do know a lot. Like, A LOT a lot. I am very worldly. What's that? No, I'm not in Mensa or anything. But I could be. Obviously. I just don't have time for all the paperwork. Or those meetings. Those are probably a drag. So, in conclusion, the only reason I are not in Mensa is because I don't have time for the paperwork or the meetings. Moving on.

I spend a lot of time listening to spiritual advisers and I have read a lot of books on the power of positive thinking. And I agree with what they say—it makes a big difference in your life when you stay positive. I am positive of this. It helps to surround yourself with positive people. No one likes to be around Negative Nellies. Try and spend more time with Positive Peters and Happy Helens. And Beyoncé. She's so pretty and fun.

Another thing you can do—and this is just off the top of my head—is watch my show every day. I try to make it an escape from the things in life that are not so great. I keep it happy and positive and upbeat. Plus, it's much cheaper than a prescription with none of the negative side effects.

It has been proven that when we're positive and happy, endorphins rush through our system. Now, I'm no scientist, but I know what endorphins are. They're tiny, little magical elves that swim through your bloodstream and tell funny jokes to each other. When they reach your brain, you hear what they're saying and that boosts your health and happiness. "Knock, knock...Who's there?...Little endorphin... Little endorphin who?...Little endorphin Annie." And then the endorphins laugh, and then you laugh. See? It's science.

Don't get me wrong. Everyone has good days and bad days. We're humans. We have emotions. In fact, I don't trust anyone who doesn't have emotions. Have you ever met someone who says they've never had a bad day in their whole entire life? Don't you want to poke them in the face? I don't understand people like that. We all wake up on the wrong side of the bed some days. Some days we even wake up on the wrong side of our neighbor's driveway because of a late night out and some confusion over strikingly similar front doors. My point is, life is about balance. The good and the bad. The highs and the lows. The piña and the colada.

The thing everyone should realize is that the key to happiness is being happy by yourself and for yourself. If everything you have got stripped away—your home, your job, your family, your things, your favorite T-shirt with all the holes in it that you won't throw away even though it reveals a large part of your stomach region—if you lost all of those things and you had to live in a cave all alone with absolutely nothing, you should still be happy. Happiness comes from within. You have the power to change your own mind-set so that all the negative, horrible thoughts that try to invade your psyche are replaced with happy, positive, wonderful thoughts.

I myself have made a conscious choice to not allow negative thoughts to even enter my mind. Is it hard? You bet it is. Negative thoughts are powerful. For example, if I didn't make that commitment to myself to think positively all the time, I would probably start thinking about how scary it would be to live in a cave all alone with absolutely nothing. Because I mean, if I really think about the reality of that situation, it's terrifying—to be trapped in a cave with all those bats flying around everywhere. And the spiders! There are probably literally millions and millions of spiders in caves. I don't have anything against bats and spiders. Especially if they're happy living their lives all alone in caves. More power to them, I say. It's just that it's so dark in caves. I guess that goes without saying. They're caves. But once you really get inside, there's not even a hint or trace of light. Just little bat eyes darting around everywhere, waiting for you to turn your head so they can pounce on the back of your neck like a cheetah with bat wings.

I'm so scared of the dark. I usually leave the bathroom light on all night with the door slightly ajar (notice my Mensa-level vocabulary) just so there's a strip of light. I know it wastes electricity but one time I woke up in a pitch-black room and thought for sure I'd been kidnapped by cave dwellers who had taken me and my bed to their underground cave where they would train me to move like a dinosaur and only eat tree bark. Turns out I had an eye mask on, but that's neither here nor there. My point is, I like a little bit of light.

You know, there's probably a lot of moisture in caves, too, which would be bad for my hair. And all those sharp edges. I wouldn't want to move. I'd just sit in the cave all day long and think about how scared I was to be there. I'm probably not gonna sleep tonight thinking about how I could easily end up trapped in a cave one day, surrounded by bats, spiders, water droplets, sharp edges, and complete and total darkness.

What was I saying? Oh right—negative thoughts. Get rid of 'em! I did! You know what a wise person once said? "Why pay full price for a sweater when you can steal it for free?" You know what another wise person once said? "Happiness is a journey, not a destination." Amen, sister friend!

Let me break that down for you so it's easy to understand. Happiness is a journey. This means that happiness is like a long car ride. Let's say you're in a car and you're driving to Hawaii. Sure, it seems like Hawaii, your destination, is going to be the happiness part. But really, the car ride is the happiness part because of all the fun games you can play in a car and all the stops you can make at beautiful public toilet areas, not to mention how fun it would be to drive on top of the ocean. Be happy on your journey to Hawaii so that once you get there you can be miserable. Wait. I don't know if that's right.

However you choose to live your life, just try to enjoy it as much as you can. Fill yourself with joy. (Not the dishwashing liquid.) And accept what life throws at you—the good, the bad, the ugly, the awkward, the fun, the boring, the sweet, the sour, the salty, the ripe, the unripe...I'm sorry, I have to be right back. I just got really hungry.

Magic

I love magic. I've had a lot of magicians and illusionists perform on my show and I am always in awe of what they can do. I actually learned a mind-reading trick and I thought I would try it out on you if you'd like.

All you have to do is think of a number. Any number.

Are you thinking of it?

Okay, say it out loud.

Now turn the page.

That's what I was thinking of.
Ahhh! Isn't that freaky?!

Girl Power

The bra. Disposable diapers. Wite-Out. A medical syringe. Windshield wipers. Chocolate chip cookies. Spanx.

What do all of these things have in common? They're all in my shopping cart right now. Shoot. I must have taken someone else's cart by accident. I hate when that happens.

Well, anyway. Do you know what else these things have in common? They were all invented by a woman. Not the same woman. They were each invented by different women over the course of the last hundred years or so. (That would be incredible if the same woman invented all of those things. What an eclectic and potentially unstable person that would be!)

And those are just a few of the things that female ladies have invented. The list goes on and includes things that have become staples in our everyday lives, like the car heater, the dishwasher, the electric washing machine, and perhaps one of the greatest inventions of our time, the trash can with a foot pedal. We take so many of these things for granted and yet without the women who invented them, we would be cold, filthy people with soiled dishes, disgusting cans, and unruly breasts.

I'm very proud to be a woman. I've been one my whole life. And I know that without the amazing and inspiring women who came before me, I wouldn't be where I am today. I grew up admiring strong, funny women like Lucille Ball and Carol Burnett. Barbara Walters, Diane Sawyer, and Oprah Winfrey paved the way for me to be doing exactly what I'm doing. Oprah paved the way with actual gold because she had some left over from when she paved her driveway.

And now that I have my own show on television I feel a sense of responsibility to follow in their footsteps and have a positive influence on the young girls and women who watch me every day. That's why I keep things light and upbeat and it's why I try to have powerful and influential women on my show to serve as examples for the people at home. I love having women like Michelle Obama and Hillary Clinton on my show. I also love having regular, everyday women on my show with inspiring stories about their personal journeys. And one time I had a woman on who could bend over backward and put a hat on her head using only her feet. If that's not inspiring, I don't know what is.

My show is targeted to women. I know men watch, too, and I'm happy about that. I like to think men, women, children, and cats can enjoy my contagious wit in equal measure. But overall the audience for my show is mostly made up of women. I don't know exactly what the demographics are. It's a very confusing and complicated system that only people with high government clearance levels can fully understand. But I believe our key demographic is women 25 to 54 years old. Beyond that we try to target Armenians between the ages of 35 and 80, and women named Diane between the ages of 18 and 104.

I don't know if that's right. And don't even get me started on the ratings system. From what I understand, there's a gentleman in a basement somewhere keeping track of who turns their televisions on between the hours of 8:00 a.m. and 6:00 p.m. and he writes it down on a piece of lint and then, based on his annual report and opinion, shows get canceled or picked up.

Anyway, I just want to able to use the platform I have in front of millions of people around the world every day for good things. I want young girls to know that they should dream big and that if they put their minds to it they can accomplish anything. When I go out and do my show every day I'm thinking two things: Can I inspire someone today? And will my guests have good breath?

I always think of that James Brown song "It's a Man's Man's Man's World" when I think about girl power. I also think of the Spice Girls, which makes me think about spices, which makes me think about food, which makes me hungry, which makes me need to eat a sandwich every time that song comes on the radio.

I like James Brown but that song is so wrong. It's not just a man's, man's, man's world. It's also a woman's, woman's, woman's world. He sings that "man made the cars to take us over the road." And that may be true, but what terrible driving visibility we would have on that road were it not for the woman who made the windshield wipers.

If you're going to listen to that song then you should also listen to my personal anthem, "Sisters Are Doin' It for Themselves" as sung by one of the most brilliant songstresses of all time, Aretha Franklin. She sings about how sisters are not just stuck working in kitchens anymore. They're now doctors, lawyers, and politicians. At first, I did think she was singing about one very talented family of sisters all doing wonderful things with their lives. Now, of course, I realize she meant sisters, as in all women.

Women can do stuff, too! And to whoever is listening to me or watching me or reading me, that is what I want to say. The world can benefit from more smart ladies. I like smart people. I assume most people do. I've never heard anyone say, "Boy, do I love idiots," though I'm sure people have.

Maybe at some point we won't have to break success down along gender lines. Maybe we won't have to say a man did this or a woman invented that. Maybe we'll just be able to say this wonderful, smart, creative person did something extraordinary and that will be that. But until then, I'm proud to be part of the sisters who are doin' it for themselves.

Boredom

Do you ever just think, "I'm bored"? Maybe because we're always moving at such a fast pace or because there are only so many Lifetime movies about perfect couples who aren't actually perfect you can watch in one weekend, every once in a while when we're sitting still we find ourselves thinking, "I'm really bored right now." So here are some suggestions for things you can do when you get bored.

1. Clean my house.
2. Look at your pets. If you look at them long enough, you can almost figure out what they're thinking. Usually it's

"Why has she been looking at me for so long? She must be really bored."

3. Cut up fruit.
4. Sext.
5. Make a smoothie.
6. Volunteer.
7. Volunteer opinions to strangers.
8. Hitchhike.
9. Photograph geese.
10. Put on a blazer and pretend to be a docent at your local museum.

Ellen's Guide to Gift Giving

It is better to give than to receive.
—Liars

G ift giving might be one of the most complicated things that exist on this Earth. It's
an art that requires skill and some people have
it and some people don't. The people who have
it got you tickets to your favorite opera last year.
The people who don't got you a keychain of the
letter "O" even though your name is Jane.

There are no strict rules when it comes to
gift giving, but there are some guidelines. It's

good etiquette to bring something whenever you go to someone's house. It's polite and generous and it shows that you appreciate being welcomed into somebody's home. But my question is, how long does that go on for? What if you've been to their house a million times? Do you still have to bring something? The first time you go, you bring a bottle of wine. Then the second time maybe you bring flowers. When does it stop? And are the gifts supposed to keep getting bigger? After a few years of game nights does it become, "Look what we brought you, Joyce! It's an above-ground pool!"

My brother-in-law and his wife are very good at gift giving. They are extremely polite and bring something every single time they come over for any occasion. They could be coming over because they left their sunglasses at our house and they will bring us each a brand-new set of crystal goblets. They write thank-you notes. They send flowers. And they're so great about paying the dry cleaning bills I send them after they get little specks of dirt and wine on my outside furniture.

There are some people who refuse to bring anything when they go to someone's house. Even if you bring something every time you go to their house, they bring nothing to yours. Here's my solution for people like that. When you go to their house you take something. You bring a bottle of wine, you take their microwave. You bring a Bundt cake. You take their car. It's yin and yang.

House gifts are pretty easy to manage. Where it gets tricky is holiday gifts. I don't know where you draw the line at holiday gifts. When you're a kid the only people you have to get gifts for are your parents and your siblings and your dog. That's it. And it's usually a macaroni picture frame covered in glitter. As you get older you have to give gifts to more people because you have more people in your life trying to suck you dry.

You have your family, your friends, your family's friends, your friends' families, everyone at work. And all those people get nicer and nicer around the holidays. Everyone's extra helpful. "Do you need anything else, Mrs.

DeGeneres? Can I shine your shoes for you?" And I'm always like, "Don't be silly. You should be doing that anyway."

It gets harder and harder to figure out where the cutoff line is. I always like to get something for my mail carrier, but then I have to get something for my UPS person. That means I then have to get something for my FedEx person, my garbage person, my pool person, my plant lady person, my fish pond person, my trainer, my vocal coach, my dog's vocal coach, and of course the woman who washes my face. And then what about the people I hire to do all my Christmas shopping? Do I have to get them gifts, too?

No matter what, you're going to forget someone who didn't forget you. Here's how to deal with it—take what they got you and tell them how much it means to you. Then reach into your bag and say, "I got you something special also. Wanna know what it is? Come here. Come a little closer. A little closer. Closer still. One more step toward me. I got you a hug." And then you squeeze 'em real tight until you think you've squeezed out all of the disappointment.

I feel bad for people with December birthdays because they have to deal with the combo gift. They are constantly hearing, "This is for your birthday and Christmas! Happy birthmas!" A combo gift means you get one real gift and, if you're lucky, one extra thing your friend found while she was in the checkout line at Target. "Oooh, a sweater and Krazy Glue?! Thanks!" "Well, I know how much you love to glue stuff permanently! Merry birthday!"

It's really bad if your birthday is actually on Christmas day. (Unless you're Jesus. In that case—what a party! By the way, if you are Jesus, thank you so much for buying this book. What an honor. Is there any way you'd give a quote for the paperback edition? I mean, who wouldn't buy it if Jesus recommended it on the back? I ask only because Oprah's Book Club ended and it would be a huge get, but you don't have to decide right now.)

Anyway, if your birthday is on Christmas day and you're not Jesus, you should start telling people your birthday is on June 9 or something. Just read up on the traits of a Gemini.

Suddenly you're a multitasker who loves the color yellow. Because not only do you get stuck with the combo gift, you get the combo song. "We wish you a merry Christmas—and happy birthday, Terry—we wish you a merry Christmas—happy birthday, Terry—we wish you a merry Christmas and a happy New Ye— Birthday, Terry!"

It's not fair and I have a message for parents out there. Don't do that to your kids. Plan your love. I'm not great at baby math, so I'm just gonna say in the early part of the year, maybe January until March, stay away from each other. It's not gonna be easy. Those are winter months and you're going to want to stay warm. But unfortunately one of you is going to have to sleep in a tent in the backyard. Or one of you can climb that mountain in Brazil you're always journaling about. Just stay away from each other. You can talk on the phone if you keep it clean. It's for the benefit of all mankind.

My birthday is in January, just a few weeks after the holidays. What that means for me is that I get my holiday gifts, and then for my birthday I get mostly regifted holiday gifts. Because everyone does the same thing after the holidays—they make their piles of "Keep" and "Regift." The iPod you keep. Ugly sweater you regift. Digital camera you keep. Inappropriately shaped candle you give to the creepy guy who works in your payroll department.

I'm lucky my birthday is in January because people tend to regift the good stuff first. If your birthday is in January or even February, you might actually end up with an iPod because maybe someone got one for Christmas but already had one. Or you could get a really nice bottle of wine because in January your friend still thinks he's not gonna drink this year.

But as the year goes on, the regifts get worse. By June you're getting a framed picture of your friend's nephew in a frame that says "Our precious boy." And by the fall people aren't regifting anymore. They're just emptying their basements. If your birthday is in October, you're either getting a Ping-Pong paddle or an infant's car seat. "Happy birthday! Maybe you'll adopt one day, Grandma!"

Maybe we put too much focus on gift giving. It shouldn't be about a gift or about who gave you what. We all know what it should be about. Money. Why isn't it acceptable to just give cash? That's what we all want. Let's cut to the chase.

No. Well, yes, but that's not what life is about. I do genuinely enjoy giving people gifts and seeing their faces light up when they open them. I once brought a box of wine to a dinner party at Oprah's house and the look on her face was priceless. And that feels good inside.

So I guess what I'm saying is it's better to err on the side of being polite and giving gifts for all occasions—birthdays, holidays, Flag Day. And you know what makes the best gift of all? Books like this. And things made out of money.

Pondering

One thing that always makes me happy is being out in nature. I love nature. I love trees, I love flowers, I love those hedges that are shaped like giraffes. I don't know how they grow like that, but they are magnificent!

I spend a lot of time outside every day. I love doing yoga outside. I love to meditate outside. Sometimes I even shower outside. What I'm trying to say is, I lock myself out of the house a lot.

I just love being outside. In the mornings, I take a cup of coffee out to my koi pond, plop myself down right next to my life-size garden statue of Helen Mirren, and do what one is supposed to do by a pond—I ponder.

I ponder all sorts of things. I ponder life and our infinite universe and how lucky we are to find ourselves surrounded by incredible forces of nature every single day. And then I ponder other stuff like how do mermaids always seem to find seashells big enough to wear as bras? Whenever I go to the beach the biggest shell I can find in one piece is the size of a Skittle. I'll still make it into a bra, but it's very, very tiny.

I ponder that expression "You're a big fish in a small pond." Do the big fish in my pond know that expression? Do they swim around and try to make the smaller fish feel bad because they're so small? Or do the small fish know the expression "Good things come in small packages"? Maybe they swim around knowing that even though they're small they have a lot to offer, like quinoa or an Olsen twin.

I can sit and stare into my pond for hours and hours admiring the stunning reflections of the sky and the clouds and the birds. We have so many different kinds of birds near our house. They're always chirping away, and I imagine them saying things like, "Oh, that Ellen—she's so connected to nature. That's so rare to see in a human."

"Yeah, she seems so laid-back and cool. Look at her sitting on that bench drinking her coffee," I imagine another bird saying.

And then the first bird chirps back, "I bet it would be so fun to hang out with her. She reminds me so much of Claire. Such a nut, but so sweet."

And while they go back and forth saying the nicest things about me—I mean, it's just so humbling—I start to think about what it would be like to fly around with them all day long, looking at our Earth from way up above, circling and gliding through the air with complete freedom. Sometimes I get so lost in the moment, I start running around my yard, flapping my arms like a seagull at the beach. A lot of times I'll even start to squawk. Usually right around the third or fourth squawk is when my neighbor starts screaming at me to pipe down. He's always like, "Quiet down, lady! And put on some pants!" And I'm always like, "YOU put on some pants, sir!" because in the heat of the moment I panic and I can't think of anything better to say. Of course, he's already wearing pants, so it doesn't pack quite the punch I want it to, but the bottom line is he's clearly not as connected to nature as I am.

Anyway, we have a lot of different kinds of wild animals on our property. We've seen bobcats and deer and wild boars. One time Portia was convinced she discovered a whole new species behind our house. She saw something she had never seen before that had tiny eyes and a hairy face. At first I assumed it was my cousin Nancy, but it wasn't her. Portia said it looked like a warthog, and I had to remind her we don't live on an African game reserve. Yet.

For a long time I was pretty sure she saw a opossum, but we did eventually figure out that the mystery creature she spotted was a javelina. They're normally found in desert areas like Tucson. I don't know what it was doing in Beverly Hills. All I know is, the next time I saw it, it was reading a script for the next *Transformers* movie and taking meetings with agents.

When I'm not pondering by my pond, I'm

outside gardening in my garden. (That is, when I'm not lanaiing on my lanai.) I love to garden. I find it very therapeutic. Actually, I treat it just like therapy. I talk to my plants about what's going on in my life, about my dreams and aspirations, my fears, my regrets, how frustrated I get when someone suddenly stops at the bottom of an escalator without realizing there's a whole line of people piling up behind them. I find it very easy to talk to my plants about pretty much everything. And the best part is, instead of having a therapist who wants hundreds of dollars an hour, my plants only charge me sixty.

I just read that gardening is the number one pastime in America. Well, I just wrote it anyway. Who knows if it's true! What I do know is that gardening is my favorite pastime. I have a lot of hobbies, but there's something about gardening that's different. I think it's because gardening is a hobby you can eat. You plant some seeds, you water some soil, and in just a few short months, you've got yourself enough tomatoes to make a tiny salad.

There aren't a lot of hobbies you can eat. Like, let's say you love to cook. That's a bad example. Let's say you love to travel, and everywhere you go, you try the food at the best local—

My point is, I love gardening as a hobby. Right now in our garden, Portia and I are growing tomatoes, peppers, zucchini, beets, eggplant, basil, and a whole assortment of herbs. It smells nice, it looks nice, and I can't tell you how satisfying it is to be able to host a dinner party and offer my guests the literal fruits of my labor. (As it turns out, these are very different than the fruits of one's loins. At a recent dinner party, I accidentally asked Martha Stewart how she was enjoying the fruits of my loins and she nearly choked on her stew.)

If you don't have a garden, I encourage you to plant one. It's a fun thing to do and it's great for the planet. And you know what I always say, time and time again—if you want to add a little spice to your life, plant some dill. And learn to salsa.

Adults Only Chapter

As I said, people of all ages watch my show. I have a lot of young viewers, but I also have a lot of older viewers. This chapter is for my older fans—those of you who are slightly more mature. If any kids are reading this book, turn the page now. This chapter is not appropriate for children. It's for adults who experience adult situations, such as eating dinner before 6:00 and struggling to read menus in dim lighting conditions.

Many adults, myself included, have trouble reading menus when they go out to eat at restaurants because the font is way too small. I know there are products to help with this problem, like reading and magnifying glasses, but I have a better idea. Make the font size larger. There should be a worldwide standard for menu font size. I've included a sample menu below with a suitable font size. You'll notice that the menu font can be large enough to read while also being visually attractive.

Daily Specials for Chez DeGeneres

APPETIZER
Organic Mixed Greens with Teeny Tiny Tomatoes

MAIN COURSE
Something Delicious

SIDES
Fresh Broccolini and Zucchiniini

DESSERT
Raspberry Sorbet with Capers

I don't know why but everything sounds fancier with capers.

Gambling Tips

I love to play poker. I play it every single day in my dressing room before I go out to do my show. I play it at home. I play it at friends' houses. I play it on long plane rides and short plane rides. Basically if I'm awake and I'm not eating, working, or training my dogs to set the table, I'm playing poker.

I used to love going to Las Vegas. What a clean, healthy town that is. Here is a fun fact about Las Vegas: You can literally do anything there. Anything. You can smoke in casinos, you can drink four jugs of tequila at once, you can try to spin yourself around on a roulette wheel while wearing only a piece of string on your bottom if you so desire. But what you cannot do under any circumstances—and I found this out the hard way—is eat almonds at a blackjack table. That is a true story. I once tried to eat almonds at a card table and I was told by the dealer to put them away because I wasn't allowed to eat them there. Sexual encounters with an escort? You got it. Wildly inappropriate public intoxication? Anytime! Having a little protein while doubling down? How dare you even think about it, you stupid, stupid fool.

I don't know how many of you gamble. How could I? We've only just met. But for those of you who enjoy a little risk taking, I thought I would give you a few tips for staying "up" should you find yourselves in a casino or on a riverboat anytime soon.

SLOT MACHINES

Slot machines can be hours and hours of fun. Things spin around and light up when you win and they all make loud, exciting noises that make it sound like coins are pouring out of the machines—even though nowadays you only get a piece of paper, which is much easier to carry around and a lot more sanitary, in case you wanted to play a game and then eat some almonds or something with your hands. Just kidding. You're not allowed to do that inside a casino.

All the slots have different themes, from animals and sports to *Wheel of Fortune* and *Sex and the City*. What is more fun than lining up Samantha's cosmos to win a really big bonus? I'll tell you what. Lining up Carrie Bradshaw's shoes for an even bigger bonus.

There's no question that slots are fun. But here's what you need to do when you're playing the slots: Walk away when you're up. You have to. Just walk away. Then, walk back and see what one more spin will do for you. If you don't win the jackpot immediately, walk away again. Take a breather. Then, walk back and try the machine right next to the one you already played. You know you should've played that one in the first place. It was speaking to you, but you didn't go with your gut. If for some crazy reason you don't win the jackpot on that one, walk away again. Seriously. Walk away, and go straight to a roulette table.

ROULETTE

Roulette is a lot of fun. Here's my tip for roulette: Always bet on red. Unless red isn't coming up, in which case you should really bet on black. Similarly, always bet on even. However, if that doesn't work—I cannot stress this enough—you must bet on odd.

Here's another tip: DO NOT place a Tic Tac on your winning number on the roulette wheel and think people won't notice. They will notice. They will not get as angry with you for placing a Tic Tac on the roulette wheel as they would for, let's say, eating a nut at a blackjack table, but they will get angry. There are cameras everywhere in casinos. Everywhere. If you think you're alone in an elevator when you decide to look in the mirror to check if there's anything in your teeth, you're not. Someone in a security office is getting a horrific eyeful of the inside of your nose.

Next tip for roulette: If none of your

numbers or colors or odds or evens is coming up, walk away. I mean it. Get up, turn around, and start walking. Go directly to a poker table.

POKER

You know what I always say. I say it every day and when I'm not saying it, I'm singing it. You gotta know when to hold 'em and you gotta know when to fold 'em. And you gotta never, ever, ever try to eat shelled almonds at a blackjack table, you dummy.

Now, you can know when to hold 'em or fold 'em yourself, or you can do what I do. Ask the other players at the table what they're gonna do first, and then decide. Maybe treat it like a friendly game of go fish. "Hey, do you have an ace of spades? What about a pair of kings?" They might say "Go fish" or they might say "Go...something else." But I think it's worth a try.

If you find that you are not winning too many hands at poker and/or the people at your table are getting mad at you, walk away. I've never been more serious. Just take your fifteen shots of straight vodka and your hooker, throw your almonds in the nearest trash can immediately, and walk away. Head to the closest craps table.

CRAPS

To be honest, it's hard for me to give you too many tips for craps because I don't understand a thing about it. First of all, you can't sit down, which is ridiculous. Instead, people are crowded around a table throwing things and yelling "Yo!" and "Loose deuce!" and "Give me four the hard way!" It sounds like spring break with the cast of *Jersey Shore*. My only tip for craps is—and it's more of a request—please do not blow on the dice. Especially during cold and flu season. There are enough germs in a casino without you getting your spittle all over the place. Your lucky blow is gonna be someone else's unlucky whooping cough.

If you find that craps isn't a lucky game for you, walk away. Take all your chips, put them in your pockets, and—I really mean this—go straight to the cashier. Ask him or her what game they think you should try next. They usually have a feeling about these things.

Finally, whatever you do, wherever you go, whichever game you decide to play—do not ever, ever, ever, ever, ever, ever, ever even think about bringing a healthy snack such as an almond onto a casino floor.

Good luck.

Timeline of a Celebrity's Day

10:00 a.m.—Gently woken up by houseboy Mañuel

10:00:07 a.m.—Quietly utter the word
"snooze," letting Mañuel know he is to
return in nine minutes

10:00:08 a.m.—Dream about ponies

10:09 a.m.—Gently woken up again by
houseboy Mañuel

10:09:05 a.m.—Quietly utter the words
"snooze, coffee," letting Manuel know he
is to return in nine minutes with a cup of
coffee

10:09:06 a.m.—Dream about ponies being
friends with turtles

10:18 a.m.—Gently woken up again by houseboy Mañuel. Fed coffee.

10:25 a.m.—Carried into shower

10:30 a.m.—Bathed, shampooed, told I'm pretty by Shower Robot 3000

11:00 a.m.—Driven to work in solar-powered dune buggy

11:30 a.m.—Greeted at work by receptionist, told I'm pretty

1:00 p.m.—Fed lunch

1:30 p.m.—Yoga

2:30 p.m.—Pilates

4:00 p.m.—Tape talk show

5:00 p.m.—Helicopter home

6:00 p.m.—Fed dinner in tree house

8:00 p.m.—Read bedtime story by author of book I'm currently reading, tucked in by houseboy Mañuel, told I'm pretty and to dream of ponies

Sleep

I just read an interesting statistic: 49 percent of people think it's "wheel barrel," not "wheelbarrow." I also read that 33 percent of Americans suffer from some sort of sleep disorder. That's a lot of people. According to my math, that means nearly 104 percent of the people reading this book right now have trouble sleeping at night.

About half of you out there are going to take sleeping pills to try and fall asleep, and I have to admit that worries me. I'm not a doctor or a mother or that older woman from *Touched by an Angel* who tried to guide people on the right path, but when I hear about friends and loved ones who are on sleeping pills, for some reason I just want to steer them away from doing that.

I know why I worry. It's because of all the stories I've heard about people who do some pretty crazy things while they're on sleeping pills—things like walking in their sleep, driving in their sleep, even eating in their sleep. Some people do more in their sleep than I do in a whole weekend.

Sleep-eating is fascinating to me. People get up in the middle of the night and start eating things they find around the house—sometimes things that aren't even edible. And they have absolutely no memory of it until they wake up the next morning and find the remnants of a half-eaten sofa in their great room.

Some people only find out they've been sleep-eating after they start to gain weight. I read about someone who gained seven pounds and had no idea how. Can you imagine waking up one day full of pudding and having to ask your spouse, "Honey, quick question—did we go on a ten-day cruise last night?"

Sleep is one of the most important things we

need to stay happy and healthy, and being the type of person that I am, I want to help each and every one of my sleep-deprived readers in any way I can. I thought of some things you can do to get to sleep without drugs. So if you, dear reader, are one of the millions of sufferers, please read on while I attempt to cure you.

Now, some of you are probably reading this book in bed to try and fall asleep. Silly! Unless you get tired from laughing too hard, this isn't the kind of book that's going to knock you out. You need to read something boring, like a story written by Harry Connick Jr. or something. Or better yet, a math or science textbook. That'll put you right out. But by the time you find one of those lying around your house, it's gonna be midnight. Plus, I don't want you to have to get up from bed right now. You'll end up tripping over a lamp cord on your way to the bookshelf. The cord will knock over the lamp, causing the lightbulb inside to shatter into a million pieces. You'll keep walking, trying to avoid all the glass but how can you, it's all tiny, tiny shards scattered about a shag rug. So you'll accidentally step on a piece and you'll scream, "Shoot!" because your New Year's resolution was to curse less and, even though it's hard, you've managed to hold pretty true to your word. Except for that one time when you jammed your finger in the car window outside church and you yelled such a specific, horrible series of expletives that you actually had to stop going to that church and go to the one in the neighboring town.

After you yell "Shoot!" your wife or husband or son or daughter will wake up from all the commotion. Your son was probably awake anyway because he just got home after sneaking out of the house to meet his friends in the mall parking lot. That's always been your greatest fear. You worry that he goes there to cause mischief but really he's a good kid who just wants to fit in and hang out with his friends. He's actually never even touched a cigarette let alone smoked one, or smoked anything for that matter. I mean, one time he tried cocaine but that was only because his friends told him it was sugar and who doesn't love sugar? Especially after sleeping with a hooker. I'm not saying your son slept with a hooker, I'm just saying everyone loves sugar.

So your son runs into the living room to see what happened. He finds you clutching your foot, which is bleeding from the glass, muttering curses under your breath. It's actually a nice moment because he gets you some ice and asks if you're okay. You tell him you are and you ask him if you can borrow one of his algebra textbooks because you're having trouble sleeping. Turns out he's a senior in high school and he hasn't taken algebra in three years, he takes calculus now. He gets upset that you don't know anything about him, yells something about his "real dad," and storms out of the house. But he never tells you where his calculus books are, so you're back to square one, only worse off because of the glass in your foot and the sadness in your heart.

So what I've done for you is included some math equations here in this chapter. You just have to read them and you'll be dreaming of rainbows or puppies or being naked in English class in no time at all.

$E=MC^2$. Are you still awake?

The square root of 144 is 12. Still up?

If a train carrying cargo pants is traveling due east at 50 miles an hour and a bus carrying bananas is traveling north at 60 miles an hour, how much wood would a woodchuck chuck if a woodchuck could chuck wood? Have you fallen asleep yet?

Okay, if that didn't do the trick, I have more help to offer. People love to count sheep to go to sleep. But that can be hard, too, because you have to get out of bed, find a reputable shepherd in your area, and hope they can deliver you over 109 sheep on a moment's notice. So what I'm going to recommend instead is that you count—stay with me—imaginary sheep. Yep, that's why they pay me the big bucks. For ideas like that.

Let's do it together. One. Two. Three. Four. Five. Six. Seven. Eight. Nine. Ten. Eleven. Fourteen. Twenty. Twenty-one. Twenty-two. Forty-eight. You know what, I'm not great at counting. Let's move on.

I have one more idea. This will work best

if you pretend I'm hovering over your face swinging a pocket watch from side to side. Stare straight ahead. You're getting very sleeeeeeepy. Verrrrrryyyyy sleeeeeepyyyyyyyyyy. Verrrrryyyyyy—wait! WAKE UP! I just realized something very important. I don't want you waking up in the morning, going to work, and telling people you fell asleep last night reading my book. That would be horrible! What would they think?! They would think my book is boring and dull. I can't have that. Wake up! Go get yourself a cup of coffee, pour some Red Bull in it, splash some cold water on your face, and read on!

Letter to Mall Security

To Whom It May Concern:

I am writing in regard to your letter dated March third where you cite my potential involvement in what your company has deemed the "Vase Breaking Incident."

First of all, kudos to your team for tracking me down so quickly using, I assume, only my license plate number. I assure you I was not "fleeing the scene" as your letter indicated. I was simply on my way to an appointment I suddenly remembered I had. And the reason you may have heard the words "See ya, suckers" as

I drove away was because I happened to have a song playing in my car with the lyrics "See ya, suckers, bye-bye, mall cops, try and get me if you can."

I am willing to admit that it was in fact me riding around the mall on the Segway I borrowed from a mall security officer. I would like to offer my sincerest apology for the chaos that ensued.

It was never my intention to ride the Segway all the way through the mall, up the escalator in Macy's, down the escalator in JCPenney, around the parking lot, and into the kitchen of the Cheesecake Factory. I thought I was taking it back to mall security headquarters, which I realize now is inside the mall under the sign that says "Mall Security Headquarters" and not inside the Dumpster outside the restaurant.

As for the vase, I did not break it and I'm happy to explain how it ended up shattered all over the floor of Pottery Barn. What happened was, after I did a bit of shopping in the mall, I was tired and decided to sit down inside the Pottery Barn store on the second level. They have the most comfortable sofas by far. I must have dozed off and about an hour or so later, I felt a tap on my shoulder. When I sprang up off the sofa, the reason I punched the Pottery Barn employee in the face was because at that time I was having a dream about being a pro boxer and fighting Mike Tyson inside a Crate & Barrel. Weird, I know, since I was actually, as I stated earlier, inside a Pottery Barn.

The employee—I think his name was Jon or Joe or Wisconsin; I don't know, everyone's got weird names nowadays— asked me to leave the store because I wasn't buying anything and other customers wanted to try out the sofa. He was rude and I told him how I felt.

Just then my phone rang. It was a friend of mine named Carol who I hadn't talked to in months and months. She had some very exciting news to share about a promotion at work. I won't go into the specifics, but she's been working in the sales department of a large telecommunications company for almost twenty-three years and she's been waiting for a promotion for a long, long time. They've had cutbacks over the years and it's a hard time right now because so many people are switching to cell phones. Do you know that barely anyone has a landline anymore? Carol is a landline specialist. I don't know if that's her exact title, but that's her department. I always feel a little guilty when she has to call me on my cell phone, like it's a direct attack on what she does for a living. She doesn't feel that way. We've talked about it before and she has no problem with it, it's just something I always think about. But it's conversations like that, where you really get stuff out in the open, that make friendships stronger.

So when Carol told me about her big promotion to vice president or president or something of the entire company— I'm not sure which, it's very hard to hear inside a mall—I got so excited I started jumping up and down on the sofa. Well, that apparently knocked some cushions off, which in turn knocked into a vase, which in turn fell on the floor and shattered. I don't know who designs your stores, but carpeting might be a good idea if you're going to have fragile objects on display that can fall and break into thousands of pieces when someone does something as benign as jumping on a sofa.

So anyway, as you can see this is Carol's fault. I'm happy to send you her phone number and address so you can send her a copy of the bill. I will be forwarding my invoice on to her as well.

Now, the reason I ran as fast as I could out of the store at the exact moment Carol made me smash the vase was because, as you may recall, Wisconsin had asked me to leave. And after I ran out of the store, the reason I kneeled down behind that mall kiosk until Wisconsin passed me by was because I saw a beautiful hat that I thought might fit my head. I don't know if you like hats, but that kiosk has so many to choose from. I have a small head and it's hard for me to find hats, so when I see a few that might work I have to stop.

When Wisconsin finally caught up to me—and good for him for recognizing me under that big sun hat and oversize sunglasses—the reason I spoke with a French accent and pretended not to understand him was because I was practicing for a part I'm playing in a French movie called *Le Mysterious Lady*.

I really like to get into my roles even when I'm practicing and that's why I quickly grabbed the Segway from the security guard who started to approach us. You know how every French film has an exciting getaway scene where a car drives down a long set of steps? That's what I was trying to emulate when I took the Segway down that escalator. I realize now that was very dangerous and it was unfortunate timing that I yelled that minute-long series of very adult words just as those children were leaving the Build-A-Bear Workshop. But you have to admit the way they repeat those words in their tiny little voices is adorable.

As for the money I took out of the mall fountain, that's a much simpler explanation. After the commotion at Pottery Barn and the Segway chase and my purely coincidental makeover into a geisha at the makeup counter at Bloomingdale's, I stood next to the fountain to take a breather. I saw some children making wishes and throwing money into it and I happened to tell them that the more money they throw in, the more likely it is that their wishes will come true. I mean, a penny doesn't get you anything nowadays and kids need to learn that lesson. It was my understanding that any money they threw in the fountain that exceeded one cent then belonged to me. I definitely didn't realize that my getting in the fountain to claim my money would result in such an intense underwater handstand competition between so many people.

I realize that you still might be interested in pressing charges, but I have to say if it wasn't for all the stress Carol caused by breaking the vase, none of this would have happened.

Sincerely and fondly,
Ellen

PS—If you're wondering how three of the horses from the carousel next to the food court ended up in my backyard, I am happy to explain that in a separate letter.

How to Become a Billionaire

1. Make a lot of money.
2. Don't spend it.

5 Extremely Easy Ways
to Make a Lot of Money

1. Win the Mega Millions jackpot.
2. Create a social networking site that every single person on Earth and elsewhere wants to join.
3. Write a hit song using the word "love" and the phrase "I remember." People go crazy for songs about love and memories.
4. Write a wildly successful series of novels about magical teenage vampire hobbits.
5. Have a major Hollywood studio turn novels about aforementioned magical teenage vampire hobbits into a gigantic motion picture franchise.

There. Easy.

Inside My Head

I'm on vacation right now. Or as some people say, I'm on holiday. Or as other people say, I'm paying a lot of money to sit on a beautiful beach and do nothing but eat, sleep, and eat. I've had a pretty busy couple of years and this is the first time in a long time that I can take a break and just sit down, relax, and think about nothing. I'm just gonna let my mind wander. I'm gonna sit here and stare at the water and, even though it sounds irresponsible, I'm going to let my mind just go off on its own...walk away...wherever it wants to go...totally unsupervised.

Here we go.

Ahhhhhhhhhhh. This feels nice. The ocean

breeze is like Mother Nature softly blowing in my face. Usually I don't like it when people blow right in my face, especially if they've just smoked a cigarette or had some coffee or a bite of Gouda, but this is nice.

The ocean is beautiful. It's crystal blue. Almost turquoise, or aquamarine. Aqua. Hmm. "Aqua" is only one letter away from "*agua*," which is Spanish for "water." I wonder if that's on purpose. The *agua* is aqua. That's fun to say. Oops, I just said that out loud. The gentleman next to me just glared at me. I'm sorry, sir. I'm sorry that I'm so smart and I know that "*agua*" means "water" in Spanish. I also know how to say "hello" in Spanish. I can't remember it right now, but I'll think of it in a minute. So take that, sir.

There's someone walking by in flip-flops. That looks uncomfortable—she's kicking up sand everywhere. She's gonna find sand in places she didn't even know she had later. I bet it'll end up in her bed. I can just picture her turning over in the middle of the night after having a dream about Goldie Hawn chasing her down a spiral staircase in Guadalajara and she'll get a face full of sand. Maybe she wants that. Sand can be exfoliating.

I wonder who invented the flip-flop. It must've been someone who loves joint pain or hates getting places quickly. I hope that lady's not in a hurry because she is not going anywhere fast. She might as well be wearing high heels. I don't know if I've ever actually seen anyone wearing high heels and a bathing suit on the beach. I've seen it on *The Price Is Right*, that's for sure. Plinko is such a fun game.

We inflict a lot of pain on ourselves, don't we? We walk in high heels and wear flip-flops. Just a thin piece of rubber with a plastic strap jammed between our toes. That's acceptable to us as footwear. We get bikini waxes. We pinch ourselves when things are going well. Why can't we just be hairy and wear sensible shoes and kiss ourselves all over when we're happy? I guess that's what a hippy is. I should move up north and become a hippy.

Shoot, I can't. I have a dentist appointment next week.

Ahhhhhhhh. I'm just gonna close my eyes for a second.

That sandbar incident was embarrassing. I wish I had asked more questions before I swam out there. It's called a sandbar. Surely I'm not the first person to swim out there and expect a dolphin to make me a mai tai. They should just call it a lump of sand in the middle of the ocean instead of a sandbar. Stupid ocean. Whatever. I'm over it.

I mean, I wouldn't point and laugh at someone if I sent them to a koi pond and they expected the pond to be shy. It sounds like "coy" pond. Whatever. I'm over it for real this time.

Ooh, I feel something on my arm. I hope it's not a squirrel. Nope. It's an ant. That's sweet. Hi, ant.

I wonder why we call people antsy. Ants don't seem to be antsy. If anything, the way they build their tiny little ant huts, they seem very patient and calm. And why is having ants in your pants an expression? I'm sure someone had something else in his or her pants that was just as bothersome before anyone had ants in their pants. Why isn't it flies in your pants or breadcrumbs in your pants or porcupines in your pants? That would be annoying, too. Poor ants. They really get the what-for just because their name rhymes with "pants."

I should call my aunt.

Boats are pretty. That boat is stopping near that sandbar. Probably expecting to get some drinks. Idiots. They don't serve drinks there. It's just a strip of sand.

You know what's a funny word? "Palm frond." "Frond" is a funny word. I wish I had a friend named Frond. This is my friend Frond. This is Frond, my friend. Uh-oh, I said that out loud, too. Now that man is really looking at me. He thinks I'm crazy. The gall of that man to think I'm crazy for talking out loud. I'm not crazy. I'm sure he's had the same kind of thoughts. I bet he wishes he had a friend named Frond.

I'm just gonna smile at him. Nope, I shouldn't have done that. I think I have some brownie stuck to my front tooth. Now he thinks I'm really crazy for talking out loud and missing a front tooth. It's not like talking out loud and missing a tooth makes you crazy. There are a lot of things that make you crazy, like pushing around a shopping cart all day. I don't want to label people but usually someone who is not completely balanced has a shopping cart.

Actually, that's a smart idea. I should get a shopping cart. What a great invention that is. I don't carry a purse. I usually put everything I need in my pockets. But it might be fun to push a shopping cart around. I'd put so much stuff in there. People would be like, "Did you just come from the grocery store?" And I'd be like, "No, you fool, this is my purse on wheels." That's what I'd call it—a purse on wheels. Or POW. No, I guess I can't call it that. I don't want people thinking I'm pushing around a prisoner of war. But maybe if I add an exclamation mark like POW! people would pronounce it like "Wow," but "Pow!" I don't know. I guess it would be hard to get it in my car anyway, my purse on wheels. Oh well.

Hola. That's how you say hello in Spanish. I knew it would come to me. See, I'm not crazy, sir! Whoops. I said that out loud.

Romance: A Short Short Story

Levar and Belinda felt an immediate attraction to one another the moment their eyes met at the Aerosmith reunion tour concert. It was as if they'd known each other their whole lives. They ran to Belinda's house because it was closer, and they embraced. Was it wrong? Or was it the most right thing ever? They cuddled by the fire, his hand upon her thigh, and talked of their future. Then they did stuff to each other all night long.

Dreams

I am fascinated by people's dreams. Not dreams like, "I wanna be a pilot when I grow up!" Those are stupid and boring. I mean the dreams you have when you go to sleep at night. Or—because I don't mean to exclude anybody—if you're an owl reading this, the dreams you have when you go to sleep during the day.

Dreams are supposed to represent things going on in our subconscious mind. And I don't know how you feel about it, but that terrifies me. What in the world can be going on in my subconscious mind that makes me dream I'm a loom worker living in Albuquerque in the house I grew up in with Jamie Lee Curtis, three lions, and Kermit the Frog? Actually, never mind. I don't want to know.

I realize I just forced you to read a description of one of my dreams. I know it can be annoying when your friends make you listen to their dreams, so I don't usually do that to people. I'm sure y'all have crazy dreams of your own to analyze and I'm not here to burden you with mine! That would be really, really annoying.

Except last night I did have a dream you should hear about because you were in it. I know that sounds crazy, but you were. You. Yes, you. Don't look over your shoulder. I mean, you you. The reader. You and I were ice-skating in Germany with the pope and Colonel Sanders. Crazy, right? I know! I had no idea they hung out together. Colonel Sanders wasn't a very good ice-skater and he kept falling down. But the pope was amazing—he kept doing these figure eights that were truly Olympic caliber. I asked him if he'd ever be interested in joining my ice hockey league. In my dream I was in an ice hockey league. It was very surprising because in real life I've never stepped foot on an ice-skating rink. It's not that I can't skate, I just don't like to be that cold. And also I can't skate.

The pope said he was interested but I have to be honest—it felt like one of those "Yeah... sure...I'll call you to talk about it" answers. But I understood. He's the pope.

Anyway, at one point I noticed you had some sauerkraut on your lip, so I said, "You have some sauerkraut on your lip." And you were like, "Here?" And I was like, "No, other side." So you tried to remove it with your tongue, but when your tongue came out of your mouth it was about three feet long, like some reptile. And then—and then—you turned into a Komodo dragon. You know, those big lizards you find on islands near Japan. So I start to think, "Oh great. How am I gonna get these ice skates off of this Komodo dragon and return them?" because they were rented and I had left a ten-dollar deposit. And at that point I wasn't sure if you were a Komodo dragon and still my friend or just a real Komodo dragon—and Komodo dragons are poisonous, not to mention how strong their tails are. So I said, "Betsy"—Is that your name? Well, it was in the dream. Anyway, I said "Betsy" to find out if you knew you were a Komodo dragon. I thought if you were still Betsy you could speak like a human, even with that tongue.

Well, what happened next, you won't believe! You didn't answer me. Instead, you just started singing. You got up on your hind legs, balancing on your tail, and started belting out some old Broadway musical. Ethel Merman suddenly appeared and was singing with you. A large crowd gathered all around and when you both finished the tune, everyone applauded and cheered. People were saying, "Hey, that Komodo dragon can really sing." I said, "That's Betsy. She's my friend." I was so proud of you. You bowed and you scratched Ethel Merman with your tail, but she was so happy with your performance she didn't even mind.

Then two seconds later, somehow we were back in the States and it was the early nineties and you were on *Star Search*. You were still part Komodo dragon, and I had a special gown made for you so your tail could stick out. It was very expensive. You were a little nervous to sing in front of Ed McMahon because you loved him so much, but you sang great. You got two and three-quarter stars. Unfortunately, you were beaten by the rock group Journey.

You were heartbroken that you lost, so I took you out to a bar to have a few cocktails. We were having a great time until some drunk guy started making fun of your dress. I punched him in the stomach, and I got thrown out. You didn't even try and take up for me. You were such a bitch! You know what—who do you think you are after all we've been through? I don't even know how you had the nerve to buy my book. I'm assuming you finally got your operation to turn back into a human, probably with the money I made you. Don't walk away while I'm talking at you. Who's calling you right now? Was that a text? From your new best friend? I wonder if you ever told her that you were a reptile in your past. I bet she wouldn't be so quick to drive you to the airport now, knowing all those lies about you. Not so cool anymore, huh?

I'm sorry I lashed out. You didn't deserve that. It was just a dream and obviously I'm dealing with some reptilian issues that have nothing to do with you. I'm so glad you bought my book. Please enjoy the rest of the chapters that are probably not about you. You look great as a human, by the way. What kind of moisturizer do you use?

Seriously...I'm Kidding

One of the most challenging parts of writing a book is coming up with the title. You can't have a book without a title. You can't. I asked. And it's very important because the title is the first thing people hear about the book, so you need a good one.

Seeing as this is my third book, it was even more challenging because I already used up two good titles, *My Point...and I Do Have One* and *The Funny Thing Is...* (Why not own the complete set? Available everywhere books are sold.)

To come up with the title for this book I thought it would be helpful to look over some best-seller lists and see what titles have been successful in the past. Based on that, at first I thought about calling my book either *Eat, Pray, Love* 2 or *Harry Potter and the Lord of the Twilight Trilogy* or *The Joy of Sex Part 2: Additional Joys*. Unfortunately, my lawyer said I wasn't allowed to use any of those because of some crazy thing called "copyright infringement." That turned out to be for the best because as soon as I started to write the first few chapters of *The Joy of Sex Part 2*, I felt deeply uncomfortable.

I finally decided on *Seriously...I'm Kidding* because, well, seriously...I'm kidding. (You'll notice it has the signature "..." that all of my book titles have. I considered not using the "..." and calling it *Seriously, I'm Kidding* or *Seriously? I'm Kidding* or *Seriously % I'm Kidding* but in the end I decided to be consistent with my other books. I'm a big fan of consistency. And beet juice.)

Since I'm a comedian people usually know that I'm kidding. In fact, more often than not people assume I'm kidding even when I'm trying to be serious. That can be frustrating when I'm at the doctor's or dentist's office. I'll say something like, "Your elbow is digging into my neck" or "I think I need more Novocain" and the hygienist will laugh and laugh like it's the funniest thing she's ever heard.

It's always funny to me when people have to clarify that they're kidding. This usually happens after they've delivered an insult to someone that was intended to be a joke, such as "Well at least if it rains we can seek shelter under your bangs! I'm just kidding. I love those bangs. Seriously...I'm kidding." Here's a professional tip: If you have to say you're kidding, it might not be a great joke.

I also like the title because it reminds me of the fact that we always contradict ourselves when we talk. We say things like, "Would I like to go to that concert? Yeah, maybe." And when someone is telling a good story we say, "Shut up! Then what happened?" I once surprised a friend by showing up unannounced at a party and she yelled, "Get out! Come over here!" I didn't know what to do.

There are "well-known secrets" out there and there are people who are "so happy they could die." Sometimes people are so sad they have to laugh and sometimes things feel so wrong, they're right. Basically what I'm saying is, I usually don't know what people are talking about.

I don't know how we can be serious and kidding at the same time, but I do seriously hope you're enjoying *Seriously... I'm Kidding.* Pass it around, recommend it to friends, maybe buy a copy for your mother-in-law in case she's too cheap to buy one herself. No, I'm just kidding. Please don't tell her I said that. It was just a joke. Seriously...I'm kidding.

Last Chapter

Well, we've come to the end of our journey. This sure was a wild ride, wasn't it? I've had a wonderful time talking to you and I think we can both walk away from this experience having learned a little something about each other. I certainly learned a lot about you through the book's built-in camera that I never told you about.

So in conclusion and in summary and summation and to wrap things up in a way that will bring things to a close before we say goodbye in a conclusiatory fashion, let me leave you with these parting words: Be happy. Do things that make you happy within the confines of the legal system. Do things that make you feel good and proud. It can be almost anything. Name something. Yes, sure, try that.

Contribute to the world. Help people. Help one person. Help someone cross the street today. Help someone with directions unless you have a terrible sense of direction. Help someone who's trying to help you. Just help. Make an impact. Show someone you care. Say yes instead of no. Say something nice. Smile. Make eye contact. Hug. Kiss. Get naked.

Laugh. Laugh as much as you can. Laugh until you cry. Cry until you laugh. Keep doing it even if people are passing you on the street saying, "I can't tell if that person is laughing or crying but either way they seem crazy, let's walk faster." Emote. It's okay. It shows you are thinking and feeling.

Find out who you are and figure out what you believe in. Even if it's different from what your neighbors believe in and different from what your parents believe in. Stay true to yourself. Have your own opinion. Don't worry about what people say about you or think about you. Let the naysayers nay. They will eventually grow tired of naying.

I don't mean to tell you what to do or how to live your lives, but those are some of the things that have worked for me. And I believe with all my heart and soul that even if we try the teeniest tiniest bit we can make this world a much happier and healthier one. And if we try even harder, we can do some pretty spectacular things. I know sometimes it seems like a world that has a blanket with sleeves can't get any better, but I think it can.

Thank you for purchasing, downloading, borrowing, reading, and/or listening to this book and for joining me on this adventure. I don't mind that you dripped coffee all over the pages or got sand in the crease or almost left me behind on a train by accident. I'm just happy we got to spend some time together and I look forward to a beautiful future.

Oh, and you have something in your tooth. Other one. There you go. You got it.

Fin.

ELLEN DEGENERES is a beloved stand-up comedian, television host, bestselling author, actress, and midwife. She currently hosts *The Ellen DeGeneres Show* and has hosted both the Academy Awards and the Primetime Emmy Awards. She would host you for dinner if she got to know you better.